CONTENTS

CATEGORIES

PARKS WITH PIZAZZ, Pg. 32

RESTORED HISTORIC DISTRICTS, Pg. 33

SOMEPLACE DIFFERENT, Pg. 35

SCENIC DRIVES, Pg. 42

UNIQUE SHOPPING, Pg. 44

BUBBLING SPRINGS, Pg. 45

ANIMAL PLACES, Pg. 47

LAKE SEMINOLE, Pg. 49

NATIONAL FOREST INFORMATION, Pg. 53

MAPPING FLORIDA FUN, Pg. 54

Beaches 'N' Swimming Holes

A SPRING-FED LAKE

SILVER LAKE is the largest recreation area in **Apalachicola National Forest.** It is also the best bargain. A small fee gives you plenty of activity! Bearded cypress and towering shade trees surround the **deep spring-fed lake** which boasts a **250' sandy beach** and 65 canopied picnic tables with grills . . . Grounds are quite lovely and **camping section** is unique because each site is *secluded* and many are *under Dogwood trees!!* Plenty of cut wood about for those night fires. Favorite pastimes here are SWIMMING AND FISHING — there is a small boat launch. A scenic "twisty-turny" 4-mile paved road leads to Silver Lake.

8 mi. west of Tallahassee, FL
Off Rd. 20, south on Rd. 260 *(904) 926-3561*
Open Daily *Admission Fee*

MEXICO BEACH

In 30 years very little has changed . . . . This is its CHARM! There are the weathered cottages we remember from childhood, the **long miles of roadside beach** with "pull offs" *just about anywhere* and folks still go wading w-a-y out with floating tubs to catch their own **scallops** and **oysters.** No one resists strolling the *Free Public Pier* to admire catch of the day or flaming sunsets! Mexico beach is not "high profile" . . . you entertain yourself. I have fun nosing around little ol' **Port St. Joe** (city of 4000). Visitors have *2 new parks* with every facility. One is smack on the Gulf and the second is Canal Park which connects the intracoastal waterway with the Gulf of Mexico. Don't forget to take in **State Constitution Museum,** a 13-acre park and museum open 7 days a week, 9-5 on S.R. 71. Because of its location and shallow waters, Mexico Beach has the reputation of being Florida's *safest* swimming beach!!

Mexico Beach, FL. Hwy. 98, 7 mi. northwest of Port St. Joe, FL
Open Daily *Admission FREE*

99% QUARTZ — ST. ANDREWS

Dazzling sparkle of beaches is 'cause they're composed of **99% QUARTZ!** Over 1063 acres offer *unlimited water activities* . . . you may even rent boats in summer!! I liked watching all the "goings on" in the **SHIP CHANNEL.** This is the most popular shore park in the Florida system!!! It's certainly "my favorite"! Unusually high BLUFF DUNES topped by dense sea oats lend great beauty to this GULFSIDE PARK.

Campsites are under *cool spreading oaks* and smack-dab on the water! For *boaters* St. Andrews is "heavenly" with its jetties, piers and calm sound waters. **MYSTERIOUS SHELL ISLAND** (5 miles long) is just across the pass. A *ferryboat* chugs over every 2 hours, 9 a.m.-3 p.m., March thru October. **BIKE RENTALS** are popular as is the reconstructed **TURPENTINE STILL** near Grand Lagoon!!

Panama City, FL, Thomas Drive *(850) 233-5140*
Open Daily, 8 a.m.-Sunset *Admission Fee*

HIGHEST SAND DUNES

Sparkling white beach is no slouch either! It is 5280 feet long. *Steep dune ridges* centuries old are the tallest and most stable in Florida. Here behind protective dune line is **GRAYTON BEACH STATE REC. AREA** offering 356 acres of leisure fun. Swimming tops the list with camping and *surf fishing* close behind. A boat ramp gives access to mammoth **Lake Western** where both (salt and freshwater) fish are hooked because of the "brackish" water. Lots of shorebirds in evidence and *sea turtles nest on beaches in summer!!* In hot months a concession for food is open. Extensive **salt marshes** and nature trails are discovery places . . . almost forgot . . . dunes reach a height of 55'!

Destin, FL 15 mi. east, off Hwy. 98 on Rd. 30-A
Open Daily, 8-Sunset *(850) 231-4210*
Admission Fee

G.I.N.S. OKALOOSA

When you see a sign reading **GULF ISLANDS NATIONAL SEASHORE,** hit those brakes! G.I.N.S. runs along the gulf through FLORIDA, ALABAMA AND MISSISSIPPI and facilities are the best money can buy!!! The **Okaloosa beach** section is on Santa Rosa Island fronting on *20-mile-long Choctawhatchee Bay.* Picnic, swim, fish or lay under the ole umbrella. There are concessions, surf sail rentals and what I liked best is the location — right *on the intracoastal waterway* where you see all manner of boats from Chinese Junks to weensie kayakers.

Fort Walton Beach, FL east on Hwy. 98 (north side) *(850) 934-2600*
Open Daily, 9-Sunset *Admission FREE*

HENDERSON SUGAR SAND 6000 FEET

Price tag on this natural gem was $13.1 million. It opened in 1991 and has *208 acres with 6000 feet of gulf shoreline.* Unusual deep dune, scrub oaks, cedar, magnolia and dune rosemary make this a special seaside park. SEA OATS thrive because of the 6 dune walkovers. Bathhouses, showers and shelters are first class. A watershow goes on all day long as the large charter fish boats come very close to shore! Paved parking for almost 300 cars. **HENDERSON BEACH STATE RECREATION AREA** is a S-U-P-E-R-I-O-R swim spot!!!

Destin, FL 2 mi. east on Hwy. 98 *(850) 837-7550*
Open Daily *Admission Fee*

A 10 MILE SUPER BEACH

You won't believe it . . . there is nothing here EXCEPT (10 miles) sand dunes, sea oats, foamy waves and green salt water! This is a section of **GULF ISLANDS NATIONAL SEASHORE.** I drove the whole 10 miles and on one side is the Gulf of Mexico and on the other plainly visible is *Santa Rosa Sound* (extra scenic drive). Every 300 feet or so is a path through the dunes to the gleaming beach. Several years of reconstructing the dunes with *sea oat plants* are finally paying off. Sea oats have root systems up to 20 feet long. Bathing here is gorgeous (like swimming in liquid emeralds). Parking is on reinforced roadside. Bring all "goodies" with you — it is a long way back to town. At midpoint is **Santa Rosa Day Use Facility** *having 106 acres of developed recreation:* lifeguards, boardwalks, shelters, grills, concessions, showers, restrooms and paved parking. If you prefer, do your "thing" on the sound side where waters are more gentle. Enjoy this rare pristine shoreline — it's a shining jewel in the national park system!!!

Santa Rosa Island, FL between Pensacola Beach
and Navarre on Rd. 399 *(850) 934-2600*
Open Daily, 8-Dusk *Admission FREE*

QUIETWATER BEACH

Many generations of families keep bringing their *"little ones"* here to splash and plop about. *Shallow waters* are perfect for youngsters. Beach is 2500 feet long and excellent parking. Plenty picnic shelters and lots of watercraft rentals. The location on **Santa Rosa Sound** near the bridge makes for calm water. Come early, it's popular. Nearby the old sound bridge offers superior **fishing!!**

Santa Rosa Island, FL on southeast side of Sikes Bridge
Open Daily, 8-Dusk *Admission FREE*

KRUL REC AREA

Sweetwater Creek creates an **extensive natural pool** and since the 1800's swimmers have been doing their summer cool-downs here. *Three long boardwalks* jut into cold clear water. Shady hilltop picnic area gives mom and pop good vantage to keep kids in view. This place handles crowds!! Facilities include **66 CAMPSITES,** hike trails and a replica small **GRISTMILL WHEEL** (sometimes operating). This is a serene and lovely spot in *Blackwater State Forest.*

Blackwater State Forest, Munson, FL, Hwy. 4 *(850) 957-4201*
Open Daily *Camping Fee, Admission*

Bikin', Hikin'

FOR PEDDLERS

About 10 miles west of Aucilla River just south of Hwy. 90 is a bikers' heaven. **ROAD 259** winds through incredible beautiful hills, pastures and oak roadways. Some hills have fantastic views because they are **remnant dune ridges** where Gulf of Mexico sea water once lapped the banks. Now millions of years later the sea has receded leaving lovely distant panoramas! Rd. 259 crosses Rd. 20 at a tiny town called Waukeenah (neat) named after a Spanish lady, Joachina. In the 1800's this was **PLANTATION COUNTRY** where Prince Murat, Judge Belmont and wealthy businessmen built lovely mansions. Morris Branch is one of several streams crossed. At the town of WACISSA (postcard pretty) Rd. 59 is another scenic detour. Rd. 259 continues west for 12 miles into Tallahassee.

West of Tallahassee, FL, Rd. 259, Directions Above
Info and Maps, Florida D.O.T., Tallahassee, FL *(850) 488-7950*
Open Daily

MUNSON HILLS BIKE TRAIL

A **12 mile loop** connects *two recreation areas* in the APALACHICOLA NATIONAL FOREST. Double-ended loop runs from **Blue Sink** to **St. Marks Historic Railway Trail.** When complete there will be a series of *shorter loop connector trails.* A bridge crosses Munson Slough. Path tread is grass, pine straw, wood chips. You ride through pine timber which canopies wiregrass communities. There are shallow lake bottoms, sinkholes and natural depressions ringed with oaks. Users are primarily bicyclers but *joggers* and *hikers* are allowed too. Interpretive trail is full of surprises. 2 START POINTS: **East Trailhead** is 1 mile south on St. Marks Railway Trail, just west of the paved path. Plenty parking. **West Trailhead** is located at Blue Sink on Rd. 61. Here are picnic facilities and good parking. MUNSON HILLS is a *new trail* (1991). A 7-mile segment is open, so patience while the other 5 miles is being developed!!!

Tallahassee, FL, approximately ½ mi. south of
Capitol Circle (SE), off Rd. 363
Wakulla Ranger District *(850) 926-3561*
Open Daily (Day Use) *Admission FREE*

A BIRD'S EYE VIEW

LOGAN'S BLUFF towers to 300 feet. At Red Rock scenic vista you'll encounter **cliffs** — use caution — Florida Trail through **Torreya**

State Park is 7 miles of rare Florida geology much like the *Appalachian Mountains!!!!* Beaver dams, turkey and deer are often sighted. Along the trail is rare Florida Yew (largest bigleaf magnolia) and Gopherwood (Stinking Cedar) from which Noah's Ark was built — maybe! *High Bluffs give spectacular viewing.* I prefer these loop trails (halfway home before you know it)!

Bristol, FL (10 mi. north) of Rd. 20
Torreya State Park *(850) 643-2674*
Open Daily, 8-Sunset *Admission Fee*

29 MILES TO VICKSBURG

Passes through 6911 acres of **PINE LOG STATE FOREST** having a *swimming lake* and waters for fishing and canoeing. St. Joe portion is not single species tree farming, but a mix of hardwoods in old areas. Frequenting the older growths are owls, hawk and deer herds. Savannahs and titi streams interlace the trail. Many stream crossings with unique names . . . Botheration Creek Swamp, Burnt Mill Creek! Part of hike skirts **Point Washington W.M.A.** (136,000 acres). This long trek requires planning. Trail is *closed in hunting season.* Info: call Pine Log State Forest. West trail is at Ebro, FL at Choctawhatchee River Bridge on SR 20 — East trail begins at Vicksburg, FL on SR 77.

Ebro, FL, Rd. 20, Pine Log State Forest *(850) 547-9071*
Open Daily (Closed Hunting Season) *Admission FREE*

A SHORTIE HIKE

Just long enough to fill a lazy afternoon. The **4½ mile footpath** originates at *Krul Rec. Area,* crosses over Sweetwater Creek on a **swinging bridge,** thence over *Bear Lake Dam* which impounds an artificial 107-acre lake. It crosses Jackson Red Ground Trail, passing through mixed hardwoods and varied elevations . . . Many *restful picnic spots* to choose from. Trail marked by orange on trees.

Munson, FL, Rd. 4, Blackwater State Forest
Krul Rec. Area *(850) 957-4201*
Open Daily *Admission FREE*

JACKSON RED GROUND TRAMPING

A **21-mile** route following early path of Indians and traders also used by General Andrew Jackson in 1818. At least *5 spring-fed creeks afford clean swimming,* all having wide white sand bars. In early summer hikers find loads of *blueberries* and *blackberries* to gobble! Woods have an understory of holly, titi and youpon. In fall hardwoods offer quite good "color". Varied elevations mix with a wide range of flora and fauna to add zest to your walk. Stream crossings are hand bridges, rail ties and foot bridges. There are two shelters having hand pumps. Trail is marked by orange paint on trees and terminates at **RED ROCK PICNIC**

SITE (extraordinarily scenic). Trail starts at Karick Lake.

Baker, FL (6 mi. north), Rd. 189
Blackwater State Forest — *(850) 957-4201*
Open Daily — *Admission FREE*

Boating and Canoeing

WACISSA CANOE TRAIL

I found the **small hamlet** of Wacissa as charming as its river!! Headwaters are clear and fed from *several springs:* Horsehead Spring, Cassidy Spring, Little Blue, Big Blue Springs and several others. Complete trip is 14 miles with a current of 2-3 mph. There are many **side streams** with dense *jungle-like woods* hemming the banks. The river twists through AUCILLA WILDLIFE MANAGEMENT AREA.

Wacissa, FL, (15 mi. southeast) of Tallahassee, Rd. 59
Open Daily — *Admission FREE*

ACCESS: 1. Wacissa Springs — From Wacissa, take SR 59 south. When SR 59 turns west, continue straight ahead to the park.
2. Goose Pasture Recreation Area — From Wacissa, take SR 59 14 miles south to US 98. Turn left (east) onto US 98 for about 8½ miles to the third road on the north side of US 98 after crossing Aucilla River. Take this road north to Goose Pasture. (9 miles)
3. Nutall Rise Landing — Same as to Goose Pasture, except after crossing the Aucilla, turn left (north) onto first graded road. (5 miles)

LOWER OCHLOCKONEE TRAIL

Few paddlers do this whole *50-mile stretch* though its shorter segments are most popular. Snail-paced coffee-colored waters cut through **Apalachicola National Forest.** Geology is diverse . . . one bend hides *steep rocky banks,* another reveals *dark swamps* sporting "showy orchids". Just below Hwy. 20 Ochlockonee River flows by the **ROCKY BLUFF SCENIC AREA.** Lower Ochlockonee is dam-controlled so canoeing upstream is not difficult. Winter trips have much to offer even though you can't go skinny-dipping — there are no crowds, no bugs and literally "more fish to fry"!! (MAP Pg. 55)

15 mi. west of Tallahassee, FL — *(850) 643-2282*

ACCESS: 1. SR 20 Bridge — From Tallahassee, travel west for 22 miles to bridge.
2. Pine Creek Landing — Take SR 20 to SR 375 south for 10 miles to NFR 335. Turn west on NFR 335 for 1½ miles to landing. (13 miles) (Camping is available)

3. Lower Langston Landing — From Telogia, take SR 67 south for 3 miles to NFR 152 east for 1 mile to river. (13 miles)
4. Mack Landing — SR 375 south for 21 miles to NFR 336 west to river. (6 miles)
5. Robert's Landing — (Private) From SR 375 south turn west at sign. (5 miles)
6. Wood Lake — Take SR 375 south to NFR 340 south for 2½ miles. Follow road to NFR 338 south for 2 miles to sign. Turn at sign. (12 miles)
7. Ochlockonee River State Park — Take US 319 south of Sopchoppy for 4¼ miles to entrance sign. Turn east. (14 miles)

TUBING BLACKWATER RIVER

The absolute in "non-activity" is to lay back on a plump inner tube and drift down the sun-drenched **Blackwater River.** Average float time is 3 to 6 hours. Water depth is 3 feet, *white sand bars* round every curve, cedar and maple tower on high bluffs and cliffs. **Round-trip tube pickup** service is provided as it is for canoeing. Many folks have a go at paddling the whole *31-mile stretch* in their canoes where they camp at night on remote sandy beach peninsulas and listen to evening hoot-owls . . . although the champion hooters are on the Apalachicola River!! Blackwater Canoe Trail terminates at **Deaton Bridge** in BLACKWATER STATE FOREST.

Milton, FL, Hwy. 87 — *1-800-239-6864*
Tube or Canoe Rental — *(850) 623-0235 or (850) 623-6197*
Open Daily

ACCESS: 1. Kennedy Bridge — From Baker, take SR 4 north to first paved road west of Cotton Bridge (SFR 47). Take this road north to next paved road (SFR 31). Follow SFR 31 about 2 miles north to dirt road at Hurricane Lake sign (SFR 24). Take this road to bridge.
2. Peadon Bridge — Same as above to SFR 47. About 2½ miles north of SFR 47, turn east on first dirt road on right (SFR 50) and continue to bridge. (6 miles)
3. Cotton Bridge, SR 4 — 4 miles north of Baker. (5 miles)
4. Bryant Bridge, SFR 21 — Take SFR 23 5 miles north from Harold through the Blackwater River State Park to dead end with SFR 86. Turn east and continue to SFR 21, which leads southeast to bridge. (12 miles)
5. Blackwater River State Park — From US 90 at Harold, take SFR 23 north 3 miles to Deaton Bridge within the park. (8 miles)

HOLMES CREEK

A **no-work-paddle,** as current is from 0-1 mph. The *16-mile tour* is unusual as it cuts through varied terrain. Upper part has high sand banks, covered by heavy hardwoods. Lower sections are backwater swamplands. Many *springs* feed the creek. Largest is **CYPRESS SPRING** (first magnitude), having a flow of 90,000,000 gallons per day and caves to 70 feet . . . Here **TUBE FLOAT TRIPS** are popular. Rentals

(904) 535-2960. Dive facilities too!!! The canoe trail is sometimes canopied by trees. At times Holmes Creek is narrow, although some points are wide. Town of VERNON has a pretty waterside park for *lunching* or *launching*.

Vernon, FL, Rd. 79
Cypress Springs (Canoe, Tube, Dive) rentals *(850) 535-2960*
Open Daily *Admission FREE*

ACCESS: 1. Vernon Wayside Park — From SR 79 north in Vernon, cross bridge and take dirt road east ¼ mile to park.
2. Brunson Landing — Take CR 278 west 3 miles from Vernon; take dirt road 1 mile south to landing. (9 miles)
3. Hightower Springs Landing — Take SR 79 south from Vernon 4 miles to Hightower Springs Rd. Go north ½ mile to landing. (1 mile)
4. Live Oak Landing — From New Hope, take CR 284 west 1½ miles to second dirt road. Take dirt road north about 1 mile to landing. (6 miles)

BOATERS' BONANZA

At **OCHLOCKONEE RIVER STATE PARK** boaters have *hundreds of miles of shoreline to explore.* I launched a 19-foot houseboat here and found dazzling white sand beaches, steep bluffs topped by heavy forests, super good "CRABBING" and fishing. Endless hours of water fun are possible because three rivers (SOPCHOPPY, OCHLOCKONEE and CROOKED) all meet and flow into 5-mile-long **Ochlockonee Bay.** On Crooked River I tangled lines and wits with a 3-foot Gar — I lost on both counts . . . also found *ruins* of pioneer town of **McIntyre!!!** The park itself consists of 392 acres with fine camping, swimming, fishing and boat dock/ramp. Check out nearby hamlet of **Sopchoppy.** It's got CHARACTER!!

Sopchoppy, FL, US 319 *(850) 962-2771*
Open Daily, 8-Sunset *Admission Fee*

ICE CUBE FLOAT

Florida's *most scenic* paddle stream!! **COLDWATER CREEK trail** is 18 miles . . . I've canoed most of it. You'll need a steel will to swim in this *spring-fed* creek but once you're in you never want to come out. Long, wide fingers of brilliant **white sand bars** dot the banks. Creek has a shallow, sandy bottom with brisk (3 mph) current. Stream passes under bridges, floats by steep banks topped by hardwood forest . . . In my book the Coldwater is "standout" canoeing!!

Milton, FL, Off Rd. 87 or Hwy. 4 *Rentals: (850) 623-6197*
Open Daily *1-800-239-6864*

ACCESS: 1. SR 4 Bridge — From SR 87, go east 5 miles on SR 4 or from SR 191, go west 5 miles on SR 4 to bridge over Big Coldwater Creek.
2. Coldwater Recreation Area — From Munson, take SR 191 southwest for 2¾ miles to dirt road on right (west side of Juniper Creek). Turn west for 5 miles to Jernigan Bridge. Or, from Berrydale, take SR 4 east for 2

miles to paved road. Turn south for 4 miles to bridge. (4 miles)
3. Berrydale Bridge — From SR 87, take Springhill Rd. east to bridge. (5 miles)
4. Tomahawk Landing — From SR 87, take Springhill Rd. east to Tomahawk Landing sign, then south to landing. (4 miles)
5. Old Steel Bridge — From SR 191, take SR 87-A north 2 miles. Turn east and cross railroad tracks; turn north and continue to end of pavement. Then turn east on dirt road to bridge. (2 miles)
6. SR 191 Bridge — (3 miles)

BIG LAGOON

It is a *long drive* by car to this 698-acre **STATE REC. AREA.** I boated *Big Lagoon* for 8 years and found this was the most enjoyable way to see its natural charms. Location on the *Intracoastal Waterway* gives access to hundreds of secluded sandy spots (deep or shallow) for bathing, picnics or lazing about. Waters on south side extend to *pristine* **Perdido Key** which offers super exploring shores and mighty fine catch-em-yourself crab dinners. Main section on north side is ultra modern with all facilities: bathhouses, swim areas, shelters, grills, boat ramp, observation tower or fishing. There is a 500-seat **AMPHITHEATER CENTER** with stage, dining, meeting area and adjoining kitchen used for weddings, banquets, concerts or social gatherings — and CAMPING too.

Pensacola, FL, 10 miles west SR 292 *(850) 492-1595*
Open Daily, 8-Sunset *Admission Fee*

UNKNOWN CANOE TRAILS

The following is a list of less-used canoe streams — I've paddled 4 of the 7. Each has its special character!! More info and **MAPS:**
Write — Dept. of of Natural Resources
Div. of Recreation and Parks
3900 Commonwealth Blvd.
Tallahassee, FL 32399-3000
(850) 487-4784

Sweetwater/Juniper Creeks — Sweetwater Creek is narrow and swift with winding curves, but after it joins Juniper Creek, the curves become gentler and the creek widens. Spring runs trickle into this clear stream. The water level fluctuates rapidly after heavy rains.

Wakulla River — The four-mile trail on this beautiful cypress-lined river makes an unhurried half-day trip. The slow current makes a round-trip easy so you will not have to shuttle. Wildlife is abundant along the river.

Aucilla River — This coffee-colored river is recommended for experienced canoeists. Rapids and man-made dams along the trail can be a challenge, and they become more numerous and hazardous during low water.

Econfina Creek — Experienced canoeists will find this virtually unspoiled stream a technical paddling challenge. It flows through scenic river swamp, hammocks, and pine flatwoods. The springs that feed this swift flowing stream have cut deep canyons in the limestone.

Chipola River — Beginning at Florida Caverns State Park, this trail passes through 50 miles of river swamps and hardwood forests. High limestone bluffs and caves are accessible from the river. Some rapids, including "Look and Tremble Falls", will challenge even experienced canoeists. Inexperienced canoeists should begin at SR 167 access.

Yellow River — The upper portion of the Yellow River is a fast flowing stream draining the Western Highlands and Florida's highest elevation. Hardwood forests and high sandy banks frame the river. As you move downstream, the river deepens and slows as it passes through cypress and gum swamps. Part of the trail borders Eglin AFB, and a base recreational permit is required.

Shoal River — A nature lover's dream, the Shoal River threads its way through northwest Florida wilderness. This narrow river passes by high sandy hills and broad sand bars. The surrounding forest is a mixture of maple, birch, oak, gum and cypress. This scenic river is a welcome escape from civilization.

Botanical Gardens

MACLAY GARDENS AND HOME

Velvet-white dogwoods, redbud and towering oaks wear their best "dress-up" in SPRING. **CAMELLIA** (100 types) dominate where green rolling hills and tranquil **Lake Hall** are backdrops for a *masterpiece of floral architecture.* In 1923 Maclay began planting his seeds. Now they occupy the best part of 308 acres. Over 60 species include Azaleas, Camellias and many exotic flora! Blooming is DECEMBER THRU APRIL!!! The **Maclay home** is furnished as when the family lived there. There is *swimming, boating and picnicking on grounds.* Home is open January through April.

Tallahassee, FL, 3540 Thomasville Rd. — *(850) 487-4556*
Open Daily, 8 a.m.-Sunset — *Admission Fee*

A 60-YEAR-OLD BEAUTY QUEEN

Old things generally become tarnished with age. Not so with **BELLINGRATH GARDENS** and **HOME.** In 1932 Coca Cola bottling pioneer Bellingrath opened his magnificent floral estate to the public. Here are **65 landscaped acres** with **840 more** designated as a *bird sanctuary* on the FOWL RIVER. No poet could do this garden justice so I simply list the facts: Rose Garden, Bridal Garden, Mirror Lake, Rock Vista, River Pavilion, East Terrace, Grotto, Formal Garden, Exotica Conservatory, South Terrace, Mirror Lake Dam, Bridges and Pools, Summer House and lots more. *Favorite garden spot* is **ORIENTAL** section with tea houses, moon bridge, far east plantings. Hold on, there's more — Bellingrath Home is a 15-room brick estate featuring French, English and Mediterranean styles. You'll see 3 dining areas, *Chippendale chairs* once owned by Tea Magnate, Sir Thomas Lipton, Upstairs galleries with bubbling fountains and I was stunned by the **butler's pantry** containing 8 sets of the finest china plus 9 sets of irreplaceable service plates, *some of 22-carat gold!!!* Hold on, there's more — adjacent to the home is a gallery of **BOEHM PORCELAIN,** 200 pieces, the largest public collection in existence. The *November MUM EXTRAVAGANZA* features 60,000 mums! Would I detour 300 miles to enjoy BELLINGRATH GARDENS??? Absolutely! Even though this attraction is in the "boonies" it is considered a U.S. tourist DESTINATION!

Theodore, Alabama (south of Mobile), Off I-10 or US 90 (334) 973-2217
A free PET MOTEL is on grounds while you tour.
Open Every Day, 7-Sunset *Admission Fee*

Cities
A Southern Accent

"CAPITOL" CHOICES

Just my opinion, but I think **TALLAHASSEE** is 1 of the *3 most beautiful cities* in Florida!! Wherever you travel is an adventure because you're either going **uphill** or **downhill** — for us "flatlanders" that's exciting!! The following are spots worth checking out: **ADAMS STREET COMMONS . . .** downtown 200 S. Adams, a one-block serpentine public area having restaurants, shops and green leisure places. **THE OLD CAPITOL** (daily tours — (904) 487-1902). Visit **THE SUPREME COURT,** hear the justices and lawyers cross swords (some cases are "snoozers"). Drive the **CANOPY ROADS.** These natural green cathedrals are lined with centuries old moss-draped OAKS. The 5 *official canopy roads* are **St. Augustine, Miccosukee, Meridian, Old Bainbridge** and **Centerville Roads. OLD CITY CEMETERY** and **EPISCOPAL CEMETERY** (Park Ave. & Bronough St.). Union and Confederate Soldiers rest here, also Prince Murat (Napoleon's Nephew) and Florida Governors. Downtown parking is chancey??? I hopped on the **OLD**

TOWN TROLLEY (FREE). It chugs all round, leaves each 15 minutes from 7 a.m. to 6 p.m., Monday through Friday from C. K. Steel Plaza to Civic Center.

Tallahassee, FL *(850) 413-9200* *Visitor Bureau 1-800-628-2866*

CARRABELLE'S COP SHOP

World's **smallest police station** is at CARABELLE, FL in a telephone booth. Carabelle has other distinctions. It is a river town, a gulfside town and an island town located on *ST. JAMES ISLAND!!!* Town perches on hill dunes where many cottages were built atop Indian shell middens. A fleet of **50 shrimp boats** insure dockside activity. On visiting the ancient *drugstore* you'll see the old-timey ice cream bar and tables where couples still sip-n-share "soda through a straw"! At Tillie Miller Bridge is a top-o-the-line *motel, boatel marina* with 120 boat slips. Looking for history??? A Civil War fight occurred on Coomb's Hill on Marine Street — local militia left no Yankee survivors. In 1893 over 1500 people lived and worked in the lumber industry which supported hotels, wharves and a railroad station. In 1916 GREEK SPONGE DIVERS carried on a lively trade for 8 years. East of Carabelle during World War II Camp Gordon Johnson was established to train men on **DOG ISLAND** for the amphibious landing on Normandy beaches in Europe. Offshore island, turquoise water and bobbing craft make for some *exceptional scenery!!*

Carabelle, FL, Hwy. 319-98

WEST POINT — EAST POINT

Until 1831 **APALACHICOLA** was called West Point. Oyster is "King" is this old-fashioned gulf town where *dogs still walk the kids to school.* Over 192,000 acres make up the **river basin** which produces 90% of Florida oysters!! A delightful town for "rubbernecking" as avenues are wide with little traffic. Homes on BAY STREET are *grandly preserved.* There is Gothic Revival, Queen Anne, Steamboat styles and others to admire. I lunched at a water park on 13th Street and Avenue B (neat fish pier too). St. Patrick Church, 1929, (Romanesque) and Trinity Episcopal, 1835, (Greek Revival) are two of the many churches in Apalachicola . . . One resident told me that on Sundays all the church bell towers begin pealing together and the resulting bell symphony is quite unusual!! Chamber has an excellent **walk-drive tour map** of 51 historic buildings. Elegant 3-story **1907 GIBSON INN** is the town grandame!! Landlubbers and waterfolk gravitate to BATTERY PARK MARINA — lots to ogle here! FROG LEVEL eatery is one of many yummy *dining houses* in Apalachicola. Across Gorrie Bridge is **EAST POINT** where scores of tiny shallops bob at anchor — containing long rake tongs used to harvest oyster and scallops. SEAFOOD HOUSES line the shore where day and night trucks from all over the states come to load crates of seafood for distribution.

Apalachicola, FL *Chamber of Commerce (850) 653-9419*

VALPARAISO ON BOGGY BAYOU

I discovered **"Valley of Paradise"** in 1971. It has not changed "one iota" . . . It can't. There's nowhere for it to grow as it is completely hemmed by military base boundaries. *This insures its charm!!!* Val P. huddles atop **bluffs** overlooking **Boggy Bayou.** A scenic route along **BAYSHORE DR.** reveals not homes of the well-heeled, but rather, lovely homes of middle America! They don't mind *sharing* their waterfront — at least 4 green parks (public) dot the bayou (in front) of the homes! They are Chamber of Commerce Park, Lincoln, Florida and one other park. I boated the *numerous bayous* (deep water) in the area where curious dolphin swam close to sandy swim shores. In late summer residents pick "buckets of juicy blueberries" in the nearby forest!! Bayous, Blueberries, Blufftop homes — that has to be "paradise" in anyone's book!

Valparaiso, FL, John Sims Pkwy. *Chamber of Commerce*
(850) 678-2323

TWO RIVER TOWNS
BAGDAD MILTON

Early in 1825 a trading post in **Milton** drew settlers. Both towns became lumber ports where 4-masted schooners from around the world came to buy. Deep forests are gone but Milton is *rich in its waterways.* The BLACKWATER RIVER is the **"Canoe Capital of Florida".** Jungly YELLOW RIVER, Coldwater Creek, Juniper Creek, Clear, Sweetwater and Pond Creeks are just a few of many popular *recreational streams!!!* Having lived in Milton 8 years I believe it should also hold title as **Blackberry Capital** — *each June we'd gather not pints but gallons* of blackberries (any roadside) paved, dirt, anywhere on outskirts of town or the mother-lode in Blackwater Forest m-m-m-m!! Milton's **historic area** centers about the Courthouse square. Here stand 1913 Exchange Hotel, 1877 St. Mary's Church and lovely 1871 Ollinger-Tilghman House with its old bell turn and latchkey door. More restored dwellings are on Oak, Pine, Elmira and other side streets. New **RIVERWALK PARK** is great for lunching or a stroll. Near east Hwy. 90 is a *scenic drive* around **Wright Basin** where lovely homes perch on forest hills over 100 feet high. **BAGDAD** is a *"town under trees",* a sort of fat peninsula bordered by Pond Creek, Blackwater River and Blackwater Bay. Main thoroughfare is *Forsyth Street* . . . old schoolhouse, ancient post office, a few old homes, pioneer cemetery off Church St. and a gorgeous *"bayview"* at Sally McCurdy's boarded up old grocery store!! Milton and Bagdad are rich in natural assets, but their brightest stars are the *downhome-folks* who call these river cities home!!!

Chamber of Commerce
Milton-Bagdad, FL, Hwy. 90 *(850) 623-2339*

Classic Churches

ST. JOHN'S BELLS 1880

A tall stained glass and brick tower houses a **chime of 12 bells** rung (manually) on Sundays by the BELLRINGERS GUILD. Every several feet the brick church is graced by exceptional *stained glass artistry.* St. John's is unusual because of the roof **Truss Supports!** A German cabinet maker *hand carved* the stunning altar which is composed of **5 Florida woods** (magnolia, walnut, torreya, oak and pine). The *reredos,* wooden altar screens, are equally lovely. **GRANITE SILLS** came from Andrew Jackson's arsenal at Chattahoochee!! Behind the 110-year-old GOTHIC CHURCH grows a **green garden patio** which I found specially inviting — note the Oregon Grape plant with Holly type leaves!!

Tallahassee, FL, 211 Monroe St.
Open Sunday mornings. Other times — inquire church office
Admission FREE

1837 TRINITY EPISCOPAL

Trinity is a **prefabricated structure** built in New York, shipped in sections by schooner and assembled with **wooden pegs** in Apalachicola. Two massive wood columns, wood doors and 12-foot window shutters accentuate the church's height. Interior highlights are decorative ceiling patterns with the *sanctuary done in rich dark woods.* A shiny gold pipe organ flanks the altar on both sides . . . I was able to see my reflection in the highly polished wooden floor. There is stained glass work and glass lamp chandeliers to catch the eye. Architecture is **GREEK REVIVAL.** The church site is on Gorrie Square.

Apalachicola, FL, on Gorrie Square
Open Daily. Office Open Tues.-Fri. 10 a.m. *Admission FREE*

CHRIST CHURCH 1902

Nothing fits a pattern in this church from its ornate *Spanish Renaissance style* to the rare **Pebble and Dash** stucco exterior. Instead of losing members, this (downtown) church has a large and active parish!!! Entrance facade on Wright St. resembles California Mission Style. On entering the side cloister door I felt immediately dwarfed by the majestic **64-foot DOME.** *Seven multi-hued windows* were moved from the original Old Christ Church (1830) which still stands today in Seville Square . . . Note the white floral motif. Sanctuary floor is marble with perimeter wall in gold-leaf. The Lectern is marked by a rich carved wooden eagle. An unusual **KNEY PIPE ORGAN** (resembles many trumpets) was specially *designed* and *installed* for Christ Church in 1975. It is springboard for the parish extensive year-round musical programs.

June peaks the series of concerts during the PENSACOLA SUMMER MUSIC FESTIVAL! A "first happening" in May of 1991 was the **FLOWER FESTIVAL.** Every nook-n-cranny, even the courtyard, was decorated with all things green and growing from Bonsai to cut arrangements!!

Pensacola, FL, 18 West Wright St. *(850) 432-5115*
Open Sunday Morning Service, for Other Hours Phone for Info
Admission FREE

Fishing Hot Spots

FISHIN' AND FUN STUFF

By golly, **LAKE MICCOSUKEE** is more fun than July firecrackers . . . and I didn't even fish! The lake is a "biggie" (5½ miles long). **REEVES LANDING FISH CAMP** is a *lively* and historic spot. Been selling "wigglers" since 1930's and *third generation Reeves* are still serving up goodies for anglers (snacks-n-such). A century old **Cypress Lodge** teeters on a hill and there's always fisherfolk "swappin lies" on THE PIER!! Walk out on the *circular earth dike* for some fine views of this super lake. May as well try your luck — *boat and motor rentals* are here. Finding the landing was half the fun. I got lost and discovered **TWO SCENIC DRIVES** . . . Try em . . . At town of Miccosukee go east on Cromartie Rd. which ends on Magnolia Rd. Go south for 5 miles or so. The path is straight out of a *"southern novel"*, completely overhung with senator Oaks. At **RING OAK PLANTATION** I expected a horse and carriage to pull out!! The 2nd drive skirts the north side of the lake. It is one road but has 3 names????? Just steer down one of the following north of the town, northeast of Hwy. 59. Take Rd. 142 or Leon Co. 0341 or T.S. Green Road — all same name, not to worry — GOOD LUCK!!!

15 Mi. east of Tallahassee, FL, off Hwy. 59
At Miccosukee, FL, go east on Cromartie Rd., north on Magnolia Rd.
to Reeves Landing Rd. *Reeves Fish Camp (850) 893-9940*
Open Daily *Admission FREE*

RIVER BLUFF BASS

LAKE TALQUIN STATE REC. AREA is one of the *hottest fishing spots* in the southeast. Jackson Bluff Dam (1927) created Lake Talquin (10,000-acre lake), which is well over *5 miles long.* Many public and private boat ramps allow access. Talquin waters are renowned for largemouth bass, speckled perch, bluegill, shellcracker and "cats"! If fishing doesn't turn you on then try exploring the shoreline. A 45-minute

Loop Trail reveals rolling hills, deep ravines, with heavy growth of dogwoods, redbud and the rare *ORANGE AZALEA*. A small **fish dock** and a **boardwalk** offer great lake views. **SUPERIOR PICNIC FACILITIES** (Governor's Design Award). Wait till you see the pavilion and rock grill pit!! Excellent for groups. There are "donkey loads" of **CREEKS** feeding Lake Talquin . . . I found these fun to poke around in.

20 mi. west of Tallahassee, FL, Off Rd. 20
on Jack Vause Rd. *(850) 922-6007*
Open Daily, 8-Sunset *Admission FREE*

GULF'S LONGEST PIER

CITY PIER is 1642 feet. It is lit for night fishing and shark fishing is allowed. A "snack shack" sits halfway out on the pier. Most anglers use a wheeled tote for their gear. Panama City is famed for fishing because of their *artificial reef program.* At least 50 manmade fish habitats have been placed in the gulf. They are charted and monitored by the Panama City Marine Institute. Recreational **DIVERS** flock to these reefs. P. C. has many dive boat charters and shops. The **United States Navy** has a complete training complex in Panama City. Don't miss a visit to **CAPTAIN ANDERSON'S PIER . . .** super dockside ambiance (dine, dance, cruise, charter fish) . . . or just people watch!! City Pier has a fine swim beach on both sides at *WAYSIDE PARK.*

Panama City Beach, FL, Front Beach Rd.
Capt. Anderson's Pier (850) 234-7437
Open Daily, 24 hours a day *Admission Fee*

DRIVE ON PIER

What luxury — fish from your car!! **Old Pensacola Bay Bridge** has almost *2 miles of parking spots* to choose from. I don't know what was running in April, but there were countless buggies and attentive anglers when I passed by. Comfort stations dot the pier. Bring shade and food. Northeast side of pier is **"walk-on" fishing** anchored by lovely **WAYSIDE PARK** having *shelters, grills and recreation facilities.*

Gulf Breeze, FL, Hwy. 98, Southeast side of Pensacola Bay Bridge
Open Daily *Admission Fee*

BEAR LAKE

Here is a 107-acre impoundment on Bear Creek. Depth is *24 feet near dam* and original creek bed. Average depth is 8 ft. Bear Lake is ultra-neat for **Bank Fishing!** About 60% of the lake is flooded timber. Catches are largemouth bass, bluegill, shellcracker and channel cats. There are **3 artificial fish attractors** sunk in the water. I saw much activity on the wooden *fish pier.* You'll find a hike trail, camping, boat ramp (electric motors only), and day picnic tables (lakeside).

Munson, FL (2 mi. east), Rd. 4, Blackwater State Forest *(850) 957-4201*
Open Daily *Camping Fee, Admission FREE*

350-ACRE IMPOUNDMENT

Called **Hurricane Lake.** I don't fish but *photo opportunities* were endless! An earth dam on Hurricane Creek created the 350-acre lake. Maximum depth is 24 feet, with average being 7 feet. Landfilled **fishing fingers** extend into the "octopus-shaped" lake. **Fish attractors** number 8, some reaching 120 feet in length. These are *hot spots* for largemouth bass, warmouth, bluegill and cats. About 50% of the lake is *flooded timber* with a large island on extreme north side. Facilities are boat ramps (electric motors only), restrooms, "primitive campsites". An 8-mile *DIRT ROAD* gives lake access.

Baker, FL (12 mi. northwest), Rd. 4
Off Beaver Creek Rd., Blackwater State Forest — *(850) 957-4201*
Open Daily — *Admission FREE*

Flea Markets

FLEA MARKET TALLAHASSEE

"Rain or Shine" the dealers are here. Over **500 booths** offering *plenty of product choices* and the **walkways are covered** for comfortable shopping. It is a large mart spreading over **22 ACRES . . .** on a good weekend a crowd of 30,000 is not unusual. Being in business since 1984 makes this flea market a sort of *"Tallahassee tradition"!* Come on out, ya can gobble goodies while ya browse.

Tallahassee, FL, 200 S.W. Capitol Circle (Rd. 263) — *(850) 877-3811*
Open Sat. & Sun. 9-5 year-round — *Admission FREE*

SARGE'S FLEA MARKET

This bargain shop has **2 sections.** One is indoors. The other part is outdoors. It is under shelter and been operating since 1982. Sarge says biggest days are weekends. Outside tables accommodate 300 vendors and indoors contains about 40 stalls. Shoppers find a good *mix of new and used items.* Certain vendors will "haggle" on price; others stand pat . . . might as well try your skill!

Panama, City, FL, Across from Fairgrounds
2233 E. 15th Street (same as Hwy. 98) — *(850) 769-0137*
Open Tues.-Sun. WEEKENDS BEST — *Admission FREE*

T AND W FLEA MARKET

I don't remember Flea Markets when I was a kid . . . we did have "Junk Shops" . . . wonder if they're the same??? Anyhow, flea marts are big business nowadays. **T and W** has a whole **10 acres** for you to amble through. On Saturday or Sunday about *500 vendors* are on scene. Sheltered walkways protect from rain or sun. *Three snack-bar concessions* serve up goodies. Flea marts are the least expensive form of entertainment I know and this one must suit the local folk as they've been coming for 13 years!!!

Pensacola, FL, 1717 North T. St. *(850) 433-4315*
Open Sat. & Sun. *Admission FREE*

Mighty Forts and Lighthouses

A FALLDOWN LIGHTHOUSE CAPE SAN BLAS

Cats have 9 lives, this shore sentinel has 6 lives. $10,000 built the first lighthouse in 1838. Wild hurricanes, erosion and shifty sands "did in" the other four. The feline 6th tower was complete in 1885 . . . It still stands erect and proud and welcomes lighthouse buffs to "photo away"!! Just north you'll find *miles of sugar white beaches* (St. Joe Bay side), where **CRABBIN'** and **SHRIMPIN'** are most rewarding — I caught enough for a meal!

Port St. Joe, FL (7 mi. south), Rd. 30

ST. MARKS BEACON

Its mighty light has split night skies since 1831. This **NATIONAL HISTORIC SITE** rises 73 feet marking the entrance to the *pristine* ST. MARKS RIVER. It is a working station seen from 20 miles out to sea. The solid brick walls are crowned by a black turret structure housing the lamp. A lightkeeper's *rather large cottage* with porches hovers at the base. Both structures are occasionally open for viewing, but not to worry . . . exterior accessibility is excellent . . . there are *lunch tables* and I enjoyed watching the boats putting in at the nearby LAUNCH.

Newport, FL, (south of Tallahassee).
On Rd. 59 in ST. MARKS WMR *(850) 925-6121*
Open Daily

CAPE ST. GEORGE LIGHTHOUSE

Since 1766 the cape earned a frightful reputation when the ship TIGER sank on a ledge with crew and passengers marooned on the island

and 81 days later due to starvation and cannibalism only one man and a women survived. British soldiers rescued the pair, bringing their 11-week ordeal to an end. The first tower "winked" on in 1833. A 2nd beacon (1847) was chucked into the sea by a storm and the 3rd lighthouse (1852) is alive and blinking today. It is 78 feet tall and once stood *1200 feet inland* . . . Hurricane Kate swept by in 1985 and the lighthouse now teeters *on beach's edge* (keep your fingers crossed). Nesting loggerhead turtles lumber ashore during summer on the 10 miles of white sands. Cape St. George is a primitive **ISLAND STATE PRESERVE!!!**

Apalachicola, FL, Accessible only by boat *(850) 927-2111*
Island Preserve — Open Year-round *Admission FREE*

EARTHQUAKE SURVIVOR — PENSACOLA LIGHTHOUSE

Yes, *quakes* do rock Florida. This *rare one* tremored Pensacola beaches in 1885, causing the beacon lens to stop. A 171-foot tower rises above deep bay water and is seen 21 miles out in the Gulf . . . I sailboated these green bay waters for 8 years and always admired the tuxedo paint job on the tower — formal black and white lend dignity and prominence to the 1825 structure. On a 40-foot bluff are "keepers quarters" converted to **LIGHTHOUSE APARTMENTS** which may be rented . . . for info write Lighthouse Apartments, Oak Grove Park Naval Air Station, Pensacola, FL 32508.

Pensacola, FL, NAVAL AIR STATION
Open Daily. Exterior Viewing (Main Gate)

FORT PICKENS 1698

Spanish, French and the British began swapping this *coastal defense site* like boys trading baseball cards. By 1829 the YANKS outsmarted them all and constructed a 22,000,000 *brick fort*. Fortifications include gun casements, dry moats, solders' quarters, mine chambers and 20-foot high bastion walls which you may walk on (marvelous Gulf views) . ... My favorite was the 25 station **SELF GUIDE TOUR.** This fort covers a humongous area, so be ready to walk, although much can be seen on a "drive-by"! Prison walls once housed Geronimo and Naiche (son of Cochise). A **MUSEUM** displays period exhibits . . . keep an eye out for Chasefield Gravestones and Blackbird March Trail!! **FISHING JETTIES** and **PIER** are usually hot spots!! This Florida Historic Site is EXTREMELY POPULAR with **CAMPING** and **SWIMMING** facilities being most scenic. (MAP Pg. 60)

Pensacola Beach, FL, west on Rd. 399 *(850) 934-2635*
Open Daily, 9:30-5:00 *Admission Fee*

BLUFF DEFENSE — FORT BARRANCAS

1698 found Spanish defending this *bluff* (Barrancas). The original fort was of earth and masonry (6,000,000 bricks). It saw extensive action during the CIVIL WAR. By 1980 the National Park Service completed restoration which required 90,000 new bricks and cost $1,200,000. Barrancas sits on 65 acres having **3 historic fortifications** and **museum.** Kids love the *drawbridge.* A SELF GUIDE TOUR winds about 15 stations . . . or there is one GUIDED TOUR daily!! Some gorgeous Gulf views to admire!!! (MAP Pg. 60)

Pensacola, FL on Pensacola Naval Air Station
Open Daily, 9:30-5:00 *Admission FREE*

Historic Homes and Hotels

1937 GEM — WAKULLA SPRINGS LODGE

An "old-world" 1937 LODGE with *Tennessee marble floors and massive fireplaces* is the focal point in the **2,900-acre state park**. It overlooks an underground river spewing out 600,000 gallons per minute into a lovely green spring. *Tarzan* movies, *Airport 77* and other films are shot here because of Wakulla's unequaled beauty!! *Glass-bottom boats* glide over the 185-foot-deep spring and JUNGLE CRUISES go far downriver to view a mysterious green lush "waterworld"! Visitors spread picnic lunches beside **WAKULLA RIVER** or . . . go first class . . . the dining room cuisine is excellent, serving 3 meals daily. *House specialities: oyster casserole and navy bean soup!!* Aside from the OLD SOUTH HOSPITALITY and the HISTORIC LODGE, I like Wakulla because of the **4 distinct SEASONS** which unfold themselves for admiring eyes!! Park office (850) 922-3633. Lodge accommodations (850) 224-5950.

15 miles south of Tallahassee, FL on Rd. 267
Open Daily, 8-Sunset *Admission Fee, Lodge Admission FREE*

MEGA ELEGANCE PEBBLE HILL

As a travel writer I thought I'd seen IT ALL!! No way . . . this **PLANTATION** is *awesome.* Founded as a "working plantation" in 1820, its focus changed in 1896 to a hunting lodge dedicated to the "sporting life". The **HANNA** family restored antebellum elegance to the main house containing *18 bedrooms.* They led in the fox hunt, loved quail shooting, shone at polo and raced **thoroughbreds** — theirs was an outdoor life!! Central to the **3000-acre estate** are 34 acres where the Main House is, and more outbuildings than a porcupine has quills — I shall name them (be prepared to walk). Stables, Kennels, Carriage House (12 carriages and wagons), Fire Engine House, Dairy, Log Cabin School, Main Garage (several antique autos), Historic Family Cemetery and so-o-o-o-o much more. House guests include the Duke and Duchess of Windsor and Dwight Eisenhower who savored the wonder of PEBBLE HILL'S gracious charm . . . Do visit, the **warmth** and **tradition** still lingers!!!

20 miles north of Tallahassee, FL, Hwy. 319
5 miles south of Thomasville, GA
Open Tues.-Sat., 10-5; Sun. 1-5 *(912) 226-2344*
Closed Day after Labor Day to Oct. 1, Christmas and Thanksgiving
Children under 12 welcome on Grounds — but Not Admitted to Main House *Admission Fee*

MINI "HERMITAGE"

FLORIDA GOVERNOR'S MANSION built in 1957 is *a replica* of Andrew Jackson's Tennessee estate, **THE HERMITAGE.** *Six columns* frame the 2-story brick home. Classic elongated windows bound by white shutters suggest a "southern character" to the home. A well-tended garden is spotted with the "horticultural queen of the South", the Magnolia!! **TOUR** lasts *an hour.*

Tallahassee, FL, 700 N. Adams St. *(850) 488-4661*
Open Mon., Wed. and Fri., 10-noon
Closed June thru September *Admission FREE*

GIBSON ROMANCE

Like a decorative table, **GIBSON INN** is the town centerpiece! It is 3 stories built in 1907 of *cypress trees and heart pine.* Comfy rockers on **walk-around verandas** entice guests. The inn in *Victorian Style* having 31 rooms appointed in the grand manor (four-posters, clawfoot bath, brass and porcelain fixtures and antiques). Rich wood treatment in bar and dining room is warm and restful . . . and as in a bygone era a proud staff bustles about polishing wood and brass to a high sheen!! Gibson is a fine place to slow your pace. Nearby is *Chapman Botanical Garden* (not pretentious but pretty) and **Chestnut Street Cemetery** is a "walk-thru history book"!!!

Apalachicola, FL, Foot of Gorrie Bridge *(850) 653-2191*
Open Daily *Admission FREE*

OLD SOUTH HOME 1898

Homesite is 10½ acres overlooking *Tucker Bayou.* **Greek Revival Manorhouse** is in classic style. Many *white columns* support "walk-around" porches and the two-story home was cooled by floor to ceiling windows. A stained glass cupola crowns the home. Builder was a lumber baron and used longleaf yellow pine and cypress for construction. Doors are of sweet juniper. Rooms are furnished with *European antiques* and 1 of 8 original fireplaces remains. Setting is right out of a storybook beneath aged magnolias, dogwood, redbud and bearded oaks — 2 oak trees are over 500 years old. In 1968 this home was donated to Florida Park System and called **EDEN STATE GARDENS.** Actually over 6½ acres are manicured green lawn and the modest plantings are mainly a (winter garden) of azalea, camellia and like plants. Point Washington Community traces its roots back to 1821. It had a large population and was the hub for a thriving lumber industry. PICNICKING on grounds is allowed.

Point Washington, FL, 15 mi. west of Panama City
North of U.S. 98 on C.R. 395 *(850) 231-4214*
Grounds are open daily, 8-Sunset
HOUSE TOURS are Fri. thru Tues. on the hour,
from 9:00 a.m. till 4:00 p.m. Grounds Admission FREE, Tours Fee

Horse Play

VINZANT RIDING TRAIL

Only four-legged horsepower traverse these **33 miles of trail.** Bring your own mount, choose the pace (canter, gallop, walk) and enjoy this quiet green woods path. In Spring pink meadow beauties, frosty white titi and scads of yellow things bloom all over. Open *pine stands* combine with *wet habitat* for your admiration . . . Bring lunch and "horse snacks"!!

10 mi. west of Tallahassee, FL, South of Hwy. 20
For Info Contact:
Apalachicola National Forest, P. O. Box 309, Crawfordville, FL 32327
Open Daily

HILTON HORSE HOTEL

N-E-V-E-R have I seen equine facilities to equal **COLDWATER HORSE TRAILS** in Blackwater State Forest!! Stables are on a grassy hill overlooking a swift-moving creek. People CAMPSITES are here too — but horses have the best view! Over **6,000 acres** offer relaxed riding through *fragrant juniper* and hardwood forest. Campers frolic in the creek's glacier waters . . . which quickly become warm because you become "numb" after 20 seconds!! Mounts have their *"own water-play" area!!* Facilities include corrals and kennels for 125 dogs. Rustic kitchen/dining hall serves 110. Sheep and bird dog competitions occur in cooler months as does classic tradition of the **FOX HUNT!** Ample room for any type production in the *pavilion and amphitheater* . . . Famed racehorse MAN-O-WAR would agree . . . Coldwater Horse Trails are "right up his bridle path"!!! (MAP Pg. 58)

Blackwater State Forest, 20 mi. northeast of Milton, FL
Rd. 4 (4 mi. east) of Berrydale; south at Firetower. Paved road
is 3.5 mi. to Coldwater Rec. Area *(850) 957-4201*
Open Daily, 8-Sunset *Admission (Day Use) FREE, Camping Fee*

Tropical Islands

ST. VINCENT — 1625

Ya can't get there from here — except by BOAT! Almost 13,000 acres comprise this gem in Florida's coastal necklace. *Botanists, photographers, sun worshippers or hikers* . . . ALL find the **primitive isle** to their liking. Here's why!!! Over 15 miles of gorgeous beach (note high dune ridge) on west side, 80 MILES of **HIKE TRAILS,** a varied eco system, numerous deer and marsh waterfowl. **Oyster Pond, Sheephead Bayou, Mallard Slough** plus 5 **LAKES** offer fine fishing or are "hot spots" for wildlife peepers!! St. Vincent is *nine miles* long by *four miles* wide. Its ownership history is peppered with Forbes (an Englishman), Alexander (general in Civil War), Hatch (Cincinnati Mayor) and a right energetic Doctor Pierce who built cottages, barns, dams, pond sluice gates and bred an imported deer population into the hundreds!!! . . . YOU and I now own these mysterious shores as St. Vincent is a **NATIONAL WILDLIFE REFUGE** . . . (MAP Pg. 61)

Apalachicola, FL, Launch at Indian Pass Rd. 30B
Info: St. Vincent NWR *(850) 653-8808*
Open — Daylight Hours *Admission FREE*

CAPE ST. GEORGE

It's shaped like a boomerang — perhaps to bring you back "again and again"! Locals call it **Little St. George** and it's the shock-absorber for Apalachicola when wild storms careen down on this historic bayside town. The **ISLAND** is 10 miles long and *wonderfully preserved!* Access ONLY BY BOAT. There is a 78-foot **LIGHTHOUSE** still operating. It was built in 1852 and stood 400 yards *inland*. Today it is *beachside!* Central island is well timbered. It is possible to see "cat-faced" pine stands from turpentine operations of early 1900's. Old camp buildings still exist at Government Dock. *Old turpentine roads* make marvelous hiking explorations. There are willow swamps, dune ridges, savannahs and upland woods. Loggerhead turtles nest in the summer and spring and fall migrations assure a variety of birdlife. Little St. George Reserve is open daily. **PRIMITIVE CAMPING** is allowed at West Pass, Sikes Cut and Government Dock. Access by Private Boat . . . Remember . . . if you pack it IN, pack it OUT!

Apalachicola, FL, 8 mi. south on Apalachicola Bay *(850) 653-8063*
Open Daily

ST. GEORGE ISLAND

Looking for an "escape hatch" but not a high energy beach??? Try **ST. GEORGE.** It is one of Florida's *longest islands* (14 mi.) but is considered unstable because of its width (widest point is 1½ miles). There is not a lot of development (about 600 SKYHOMES) sporting very little vegetation. **A STATE PARK** occupies 8 miles on the east end of SGI. Recent storms from 1985 to '87 have not helped the delicate ecology. SGI PARK is mostly *low sugar sand hills* spotted with patches of pine woods. There is a 2.5-mile **coastal hike** and *fishing is rewarding at the east pass.* Several miles on SGI's west end are privately owned. The **4-mile bridge and causeway drive** will lower your blood pressure 10 points!!!

Eastpoint, FL *SGI STATE PARK Info (850) 927-2111*
Open Daily *Bridge Toll*

ST. JOSEPH PENINSULA

Once an island, now a peninsula. The Gulf hems its south side and St. Joe Bay laps the north. "Water, water everywhere and there — IS — a drop to drink" because this 2,516-acre **state park** has *freshwater ponds and marshes!* It is heavily forested with stunning 65-foot dune formations. Note the strange pines deeply covered by dunes but continuing to grow! Furnished cabins (bayside) are always in demand. **HIKERS** love tramping the *2,650-acres of trails in the wilderness preserve.* On Eagle Harbor is a marina, concessions and boat ramp. Birders flock to St. Joe because of the 209 species which have been sighted. Clear water draws the scuba crowd. Crabbing and scalloping can be rewarding!

Port St. Joe, FL, on Rd. 30-E, off U.S. 98 *(850) 227-1327*
Open Daily, 8-Sunset *Admission Fee*

DOG ISLAND

The (toney set) has tried to retain the French name, ISLES de CHIEN but through the centuries **Dog Island** has stuck!! These 7½ miles hemmed round by emerald water are quite pretty. 3½ miles of *sand road* pass by hardwood forest, sugar mountains (65 ft. dune ridges) and about 100 vacation homes. Nearly 900 acres are fresh and saltwater *wetlands.* Wind sculptured crooked oaks and pines are roadside curiosities. Solitude and a 6-mile sun-drenched beach are why folks come here . . . Only link with mainland 3½ miles distant is **ferry service!** PELICAN INN has 8 apartments for lodging (850) 697-2839. Dog Island is a marvelous *outdoor classroom* — recent discovery was a Bonsai collection of black mangrove! Over 200 species of permanent and migratory birds visit the island. Dog Island is a true hideaway . . . no telephones, no stores, no bridge . . . ferry reservations required.

Carrabelle, FL *Ferry Info (850) 697-3434*

Museums

COOL HAND JOHN GORRIE MUSEUM

Young energetic Dr. John Gorrie really got "into" the life of the town he adopted . . . he was band director, city treasurer, postmaster, councilman, major and founder of classic **TRINITY EPISCOPAL CHURCH.** This never slowed him up in caring for his patients. Many of them were ill of the dreaded yellow fever epidemic. He devised a method of *cooling their rooms.* He later invented **AN ICEMAKER,** laying the foundation for modern refrigeration and air conditioning! *The replica of his ice machine built in 1851* is on display as are many other exhibits and artifacts. While in the city be sure to tour THE GIBSON INN (1907) and TRINITY EPISCOPAL CHURCH (1835).

Apalachicola, FL, Sixth Street *(850) 653-9347*
Open Thurs. thru Mon., 9 a.m.-5 p.m. *Admission Fee*

A NINE-FOOT HIGH MASTODON

This boney creature is the official greeter and probably the most "photoed" exhibit in the **MUSEUM OF FLORIDA HISTORY.** You'll marvel at *ocean treasures of sunken Spanish galleons.* Climb aboard a steamboat replica. Civil War exhibits are first-class!! Equally fine are displays of early Indian culture . . . Something new is the **COLLECTIONS GALLERY** which focuses on a large number of artifacts as *objects* rather than the history they represent — this was neat!!!

Tallahassee, FL, 500 S. Bronough St. *(850) 488-1484*
Open Mon.-Fri., 9-4:30; Sat. 10-4:30, Sun. 12-4:30 *Admission FREE*

FLORIDA'S FIRST ARTIST 1564

LEMOYNE ART FOUNDATION is named for artist and cartographer *Jacques LeMoyne* who sailed with an expedition in 1564. He drew and mapped the strange new shores. The gallery is in the **1852 MEGINNISS HOUSE** (National Register of Historic Places). The *number* and *quality* of exhibitions is exceptional . . . about 12 annually highlighting works by photographer, Ansel Adams; painter, E. Hopper;

British watercolors and Japanese prints! Local and regional artists and *craftsmen* also share the limelight. Musical events and **"special happenings"** often are held in the **Helen Lind Garden** containing year-round plantings!

Tallahassee, FL, 125 N. Gadsden St. *(850) 222-8800*
Open Tues.-Sat., 10-5; Sun. 2-5; Closed Mon. *Admission Fee*

INDIAN TEMPLE MOUND MUSEUM

The Mound is about 20 feet high and 100 feet long. At the top is a reconstructed ceremonial house. Prehistoric Indians lived here since 500 B.C. On adjacent ground is **TEMPLE MOUND MUSEUM** (small but worth a visit)! Exhibits and artifacts display Indian technology, artistry and spiritual accomplishments. *Gorgeous hardwoods* grace the banks and top of the temple mound.

Ft. Walton Beach, FL, 139 Miracle Strip Pkwy. (Hwy. 98) *(850) 833-9595*
Open Sept.-May, 11-4; June-Aug., 9-4; Closed Sun. *Admission Fee*

AIR FORCE ARMAMENT MUSEUM

FREEDOM has a price. The most costly hi-tech armament of the past 100 years is here. The tour is at once an educational and an emotional experience . . . I was awed!!! About **30 aircraft** are on grounds. The *"Queen" B-17, flying fortress,* is most famed. Facts: 74 ft. long, crew of ten, 13 machine guns, 3,750 mile range, by 1945 over 12,731 were built!! Other exhibits are P-51 Mustang, F-105 Thunderchief, F-86 Sabre and more plus a $700,000 T-62 TANK. Cruise missle and even **DESERT STORM** armament are recent additions. Sit in a *flight simulator* and have a go at pulling levers and switches! **LARGE GUN** exhibits are awesome: Gatling Gun firing 4200 rounds per minute and a Mauser Broomhandle is the strangest-looking gun around. **Sikes Antique Pistol Collection** boasts 181 small handguns dating from Revolutionary War. The *"Little Ace"* (3 inches), 22 Derringer, is tiny enough to fit in a woman's cosmetic case! Museum has a second story balcony where **Shipman plane models** are displayed. About 100 miniature craft are meticulous in every detail. There is lots more to explore at this museum — have at it!

Eglin Air Force Base, North of Ft. Walton, FL, Hwy. 85
Tour Info: (850) 882-4062 or (850) 651-1808
Open 7 Days a week, 9:30-4:30. Closed Christmas, Thanksgiving, and New Years *Admission FREE*

A COLLECTOR'S COLLECTOR

T.T. Wentworth Jr. spent a lifetime preserving everything from Indian artifacts, home and farm tools to musical instruments. His collection is the *largest individual one ever donated to the state* . . . so extensive it is housed in historic 1907 Pensacola City Hall. The structure is Renaissance Revival, having clay tile roof, classic arched entry and 2nd story arcade! Galleries and exhibits occupy **3 floors.** Displays date from *Colonial Era* to the present. There is a "do touch" Discovery Center on the 3rd floor which is popular with the kids. When T.T. Wentworth was alive he invited the public to tour his private museum at no cost — he would be happy today to see that the prestigious new **T.T. WENTWORTH, JR. FLORIDA STATE MUSEUM** only charges a nominal entrance fee!!

Pensacola, FL, 330 S. Jefferson St. *(850) 444-8586*
Open Mon.-Sat., 10-4:30; Sun. 1-4:30 *Admission Fee*

A DEEP SPOT

MUSEUM OF MAN AND THE SEA is owned by *non-profit educational group,* **THE INSTITUTE OF DIVING.** It is a one-of-a-kind place housing relics from the early years of scuba and underwater exploration!! Some exhibits are **recovered treasures** from shipwrecks. Selected artifacts show man's triumphs in the sea since 1500's. All forms of **DIVING** and *underwater occupations* are represented. Visitors see 19th Century air supply hand pumps, saturation *dive chambers* and Navy Sea Lab's deep dive *capsule.* PANAMA CITY MARINE INSTITUTE manages the museum and one of its many programs has been to **establish 10 artificial reef sites** off Panama City Beach . . . these habitats are the joy of divers and anglers alike!!! Noteworthy dive sites are: **Empire Meca,** a 465-ft. British tanker; **Grey Ghost,** a 105-ft. tugboat (home to sponges and soft coral); **The Vamar,** small vessel used by Admiral Byrd in the Antarctic and the **Tarpon,** a 160-foot shuttle built in 1800's . . . Make an effort to "catch" this fine museum!

Panama City Beach, FL, 17314 Back Beach Rd. (Hwy. 98) *(850) 235-4101*
Open Daily, 9-5 *Admission Fee*

Nature Centers

ST. MARKS NATIONAL WILDLIFE REFUGE

One of the OLDEST refuges in America and established in 1931! These 97,000 acres are *widely diverse* containing salt marshes, tidal flats, bear habitat and 300 bird types. I took some fine pics of the 1831 **LIGHTHOUSE** which guards the salt bay. Especially lovely were blooming Titi trees. **DIKE IMPOUNDMENTS** are open year round for hiking and wildlife photography. Scattered about the marsh are Civil War SALT VATS and INDIAN MOUNDS dating back 2000 years. **WEST GOOSE CREEK SEINE YARD** has been in business for 150 years and runs October-January, when you may buy fish . . . it is on S-367 A north of Live Oak Point. The *Visitors Center exhibits* are a must but you had best decide about the 35 miles of **HIKE TRAILS** winding about the refuge!! Fishing and boating is excellent in the briney bays but the CRABBING is really competitive — sometimes gators steal your bait . . . If NONE of the above activities interest you, then you're an "ole couch potato"! (MAP Pg. 56)

St. Marks, FL, South of Tallahassee, Off Hwy. 98, take C59 (850) 925-6121
Open Daily *Admission FREE*

FIVE-MILE PENINSULA DUNE WILDERNESS

Preserve is 1,650 acres. It is a 5-mile peninsula major **geological barrier** shielding Gulf County's mainland. *LARGEST* most impressive **SAND DUNES** in Florida are here. Hiking routes number 3: one follows *center* of peninsula, 2 is on *St. Joseph Bay* and 3 is on *Gulf of Mexico beach.* **Carrying capacity** for preserve is 20 persons a day or one group of 40. It is surprising to find *fresh water marshes* near so much salt water. Lower areas are flatwoods. Location of **St. Joseph Peninsula Wilderness Preserve** is near Atlantic Flyways so BIRDING is super-fine during spring and fall migrations. Other wildlife are raccoon, deer, gray fox and striped skunk. Hiking, primitive camping, fishing and swimming are allowed. There are no facilities in the wilderness — Pack It In, Pack It Out!

Port St. Joe, FL, Off Rd. 30A *(850) 227-1327*
Open Daily (Users must register) *Admission Fee*

WACCASASSA BAY STATE PRESERVE

This is a 30,784 acre **natural scenic area** on the Gulf coast between Cedar Key and Yankeetown. It is the **ONLY REMNANT** of the once-vast Gulf Hammock. Visitors see *hardwood forests, wooded islands,* fresh and saltwater swamps and countless *tidal creeks.* Waccasassa is so remote that **black bear** still are sighted! *Waccasassa River* originates in Blue Springs (Levy County) and flows through Devil's Hammock, reaching the Gulf 15 miles downstream. Rd. 326 is a paved road ending near a launch ramp and boat facilities. Bay boundaries are breeding area for crab, shellfish and feeding grounds for thousands of waterfowl, shorebirds and waders. A special treat in *Spring and Fall* are **RANGER-LED CANOE TRIPS.** If you have your own boat YANKEETOWN is a good put-in spot with all conveniences (motels, eateries, etc.)! Primitive Camping, Fishing, Nature Study is allowed.

Cedar Key, FL, Rd. 24, *For Info: (904) 543-5567*
Waccasassa Bay State Preserve
Boat Launch at Gulf Hammock, FL, Off Rd. 19-98, West on Rd. 326

Parks With Pizazz

SAN MARCOS de APALACHEE

In 1528 the Spanish Captain Narvaez marched 300 men from Tampa and built and launched the *first vessels made by white men in the new world.* **THREE FORTS** were raised here by 1740. The last was of stone and only half done 24 years later. The site became an aged federal marine hospital and today a tip-top **MUSEUM** sits atop the ruins . . . *Tools, pottery* and memorabilia unearthed from the forts are outstanding. Exhibits and artifacts span the years 1528 to 1865. **Indian Middens** dot the acreage. A neat **BOARDWALK TRAIL** skirts the Wakulla River which is a spring-fed stream!! **TWO RIVERS,** the Wakulla and St. Mark's, border museum grounds. In 1739 a STONE FORT was built but floods and nature have left little evidence! Overlooking the waterways are *Moats, Fort Walls, Military Cemetery, old Magazine and Confederate Earthworks.* I visited BY BOAT and found an ONION JAR in St. Mark's River dated from the Spanish era!!

St. Mark's, FL, Rd. 363 *(850) 922-6007*
Open Daily, 9-5; Closed Tues.-Wed. *Admission Fee*

MOUND BUILDERS

This is *no anthill!!* A 312-foot base rises to 36 feet in height. **LAKE JACKSON MOUNDS** is a *complex of 6 Indian temple mounds and 1 burial mound.* Previous "digs" trace this society to A.D. 1200. This **rare archeological site** covers 41 acres. Lake Jackson Indians were sophisticated **FARMERS** having elaborate society rankings. Their elevated status was determined by artifacts found in the burial sites — embossed copper breast plates, shell and pearl jewelry and weaponry. On grounds is a *nature trail* twisting through part of a plantation once belonging to Col. R. Butler (served under Stonewall Jackson). The ruins of **BUTLER'S GRIST MILL** dam and irrigation dikes can be seen.

Tallahassee, FL, 1313 Crowder Rd. *(850) 922-6007*
Open Daily, 8-Sunset *Admission FREE*

A 67-FOOT WATERFALL

Famous *geological feature* at **FALLING WATERS STATE REC. AREA** is the near 70-foot water cascade. A 100-foot deep, 20-foot wide, smooth wall-pit receives a water-stream which rushes to the bottom of the "sink". The chimney (sink) connects to an underground cave. Other **SINKS** are in the park and white oak, sourwood, beech, flowering dogwood and wild azaleas create a live rainbow in springtime!! A waterfall viewer **platform** is great for pics. Part of the 155-acre park is a *swim-*

ming lake. In 1919 the first effort in Florida to drill for OIL occurred here. The site (dry) sits beside *one of the nature trails.* Wiregrass and fern compose the forest floor (picturesque) and Falling Water is popular with CAMPERS!!!

Chipley, FL, Off U.S. 90 — *(850) 638-6130*
Open Daily, 8-Sunset — *Admission Fee*

PUREST SAND BOTTOM RIVER IN THE WORLD

Blackwater River starts in Alabama and flows *58 miles to the Gulf.* Flowing through "No Man's Land" it is *cleanest most non-polluted* of streams. **BLACKWATER RIVER STATE PARK** perches atop one of its dazzling white sand bar cliffs. Parkland is beyond beautiful, having oxbows, levees, surrounded by Atlantic white cedars. There are so many *sand bars* that you don't have to share (stake out one of your own)!! 1914 DEATON BRIDGE stitches the two park banks together. In May and June the plumpest **blackberries** are yours to pick. Blackwater is famed for *canoeing* but look out when you hit the "polar" water (like swimming in ice cubes)! There are nature trails and *CAMPING* . . . on a scale of 1 to 10 I'd rate this park a whopping 10!!!

Harold, FL, (east of Milton), Off Hwy. 90 — *(850) 623-2363*
Open Daily, 8-Sunset — *Admission Fee*

Restored Historic Districts

OPERA AT MONTICELLO

The town is named for the historic home of Thomas Jefferson in Virginia. A clock domed **1909 COURTHOUSE** keeps a "senatorial eye" on a beloved **1890 OPERA HOUSE** in *Romanesque Revival Style having perfect acoustics,* sweeping stage, orchestra pit and seating for 600 patrons. Other restorations include a 15-block area (north and south) of **Washington St.** Homes are of 1873 Italianate, 1884 Bracketed, 1833 Classic Revival, 1904 Queen Anne Style plus 1888 Methodist Church (English Gothic) and 1885 Christ Church of Stick Style . . . So much to see I took the **Drive Tour** and especially enjoyed 1827 OLD CEMETERY where **Confederate and Union soldiers** were buried after the *Battle of Olustee!!* It is possible to *tour these architectural gems* in late springtime when Monticello hosts **A TOUR OF HOMES.** Monticello perches 235 feet above sea level so when leaving I always drive west on **SCENIC**

MAHAN DRIVE (Hwy. 90) for rolling vistas and super scenes — the *24-mile road* is planted with lacy Crepe Myrtle, Arbor Vitae, Pyracantha, palms and PECAN ORCHARDS.

Monticello, FL, Hwy. 90 | *Spring Tour (850) 997-4242*
Chamber (850) 997-5552
Open Daily | *Admission FREE*

A VICTORIAN SCOTTISH TOWN

A perfect *circular one-mile lake* 60 feet deep and spring-fed is focal point for one of the **most elaborately restored towns** in Florida. This was where the "swells" lived since 1882. Around the lake they built magnificently large homes . . . they were Scotch people!! McKinnons, McLeans, McConnells. W. Bruce, AMBASSADOR to SCOTLAND, built *"Dream Cottage"*, an 1888 Gothic Stick home. 1887 Magnolia House is graced with *50 windows.* Graves (lumber barons) lived in 1900 3-story much turreted "Bullard House". Astonishing describes — **The House That Bruce Built** — It entertained celebrities during Chautaugua years. *Massive white Doric columns* are 4 feet round and other features are 5 soaring chimneys, an octagon tower and central pillared portico with balcony. **DeFUNIAK SPRINGS** in 1885 became the winter home for *New York CHAUTAUGUA,* an educational, cultural organization. They built a 4,000-seat theater-in-the-round auditorium. The original construction had 40 columns and 5 porticos . . . It was exquisite!!! I saw it before a 1975 hurricane did much damage. A small portion was rebuilt. You'll find a surprise in 1886 Walton-DeFuniak Library, a superior **collection of swords** and weaponry acquired by Kenneth Bruce!!! Around Circle Drive are scores of homes in Queen Anne, Octagon and French Colonial styles. Best way to see the town is *on foot.* Don't omit side streets like West Ave. and 11th St. (hidden charmers here). DeFuniak business district (north of the tracks) is quaint and worthy of browsing. If you prefer to see the whole town "showing out" then attend **CHAUTAUGUA FESTIVAL** in May.

DeFuniak Springs, FL, Hwy. 90 (south side),
Circle Drive | *C of C (850) 892-3191*
Open Daily

PALAFOX HISTORIC DISTRICT

A restored **44-block** "commercial heart" of Old Pensacola. *New Orleans ironwork balconies* combine with Beaux Arts, Renaissance and Revival architectures . . . Yes **MARDI GRAS** is very big here! For one whole week revelers parade, party and attend masked balls — I participated 5 years running (plumb wore me out)!! Within Palafox area is elaborate 1887 Renaissance Courthouse, 1925 Saenger Vaudeville Theater, 1910 Mediterranean San Carlos Hotel, 10-story 1909 Seville Tower, 1700 Plaza Ferdinand VII and much more. Wandering about on foot is best — you'll discover specialty shops, food and drink emporiums and even an **1888 barber shop** still going strong (210 Palafox Place)!! At the foot of Palafox St. on the bay take a turn around *the pier* (a quite scenic panorama)!

Pensacola, FL, Downtown Palafox St. *C of C 1-800-343-4321*
Open Daily. Sun.-Most Stores Closed *Admission FREE*

NORTH HILL PRESERVATION

500 homes spread over **50 blocks** make this the *largest intact residential historic district* in the "sunshine state"!! Styles are Queen Anne, Tudor Revival, Mediterranean Revival, Neo Classical, Folk Victorian and Craftsman Bungalow. Street names reflect the *5-flag heritage of Pensacola* . . . LA RUA, BARCELONA, CERVANTES, WRIGHT and JACKSON streets. **Spring Street** was my favorite, having colossal columns, curved wrap-around balconies and the most delightful (pastel painted) residences. All these homes sit atop the sites of *British* or *Spanish Forts* and the odd cannonball still turns up in a garden. On North Spring St. is **Ma Hopkins House** — once a boarding house, now the most well-known eating place in Pensacola. Served *family style,* you may be seated at a table for 15 or 2. Tables groan with steaming bowls and platters of food. You might share a table with a governor, C.E.O. or a day laborer. Conversations are lively and interesting!!! It is always busy so you may have to sit and "rock a spell" on the front porch — it's worth the wait!

Pensacola, FL, Downtown from Blount St. (North)
to Wright St. (South) *C of C 1-800-343-4321*
Open Daily *Admission FREE*

Someplace Different

WORLD'S LARGEST AIR FORCE BASE

Beginning was in 1933. Here, General Jimmy *Doolittle and his "raiders"* trained for bombing missions in W.W. II. Eglin's mission in today's world is in the Munitions Systems Division in which *testing* plays a major role. You may see Eglin's famed landmark, **MCKINLEY CLIMATIC LAB** (world's largest environmental test site). It produces temperature ranges from +165° F. to –65° F. Other sites of note are **Military Working Dog Section,** the Eglin **Flight Line** (close-up of Air Force aircraft fleet) and the **Armaments Museum**.

Eglin Air Force Base, Niceville-Valparaiso Bay
Chamber of Commerce, FL. *(850) 678-2323*

RAILS TO TRAILS

In 1837 locomotives pulled cotton and peanuts down these trails. Today an **8-foot paved path** extends for **16 miles** from Tallahassee to the Gulf of Mexico . . . It is the **TALLAHASSEE-ST. MARKS HISTORIC RAILROAD STATE TRAIL.** You may bike, jog, hike or horseback this *scenic route* — I lollygagged!!! Entire trail is *rural* skirting **APALACHICOLA NATIONAL FOREST** and **Wildlife Areas** abounding in lakes and botanical curiosities. *Horseback riders keep to shoulder areas.* About 1500 enthusiasts huff-n-puff, wheel or saddle the trail each month . . . no official count on the "lollygaggers"!! (MAP Pg. 59)

Tallahassee, FL, South of Capitol Circle (Rt. 319) on SR 363 (paved parking lot)
Open Daily
Rentals (850) 656-0001
(850) 922-6007
Admission FREE

SAN LUIS 1633 ARCHEOLOGICAL SITE

Atop this **52-acre** *high outcrop* Apalachee Indians built a mammoth council house and village. 1633 brought *Spanish friars* to begin a mission, **SAN LUIS.** A 1987 excavation revealed their residence, church and cemetery. Later a **SPANISH FORT** was constructed with a block house, dry moat and 4 corner bastions. In the 1800's the site became a **private plantation** and then an International Award-winning **Winery** run by vintner Emile DuBois. In 1932 J. Messner built a 2-story **MANSION** *which still stands* and is used as a *Museum for artifact displays* — take a looksee at the gracious curved wood staircase (no supports)!! With all this history literally underfoot it is no surprise that SAN LUIS is an **active permanent archeological site.** Digs are most often done for 3 months in springtime. So much was unearthed during the *1990's excavation* that years of research and interpretation lay ahead!! This is a lovely place to **picnic** and I strongly urge you to catch the **GUIDED TOUR** at noon Monday through Friday or Saturday at 11 and 3 p.m. or Sunday at 2 p.m.

Tallahassee, FL, 2020 Mission Rd. *(MAP Pg. 64)* *(850) 487-3711*
Open Mon.-Fri. 9-4:30; Sat. 10-4:30; Sun. noon-4:30 *Admission FREE*

APPALACHIAN SOUTH — TORREYA STATE PARK

Most **uncommon geography** in Florida with massive BLUFFS rising 150 feet above the wild **APALACHICOLA RIVER! Logan's Bluff** towers to 300 ft. Civil War Armies clashed at Alum Bluff where the *high Palisades* are topped by 2-century-old half-moon trenches for cannon emplacements!! A 7-MILE LOOP PATH skirts bluffs, ravines and streams exposing all natural land features!! C.C.C. built the tiled restrooms and cabins. From a bench on one rocky outcrop you can see SNEADS, *a town 15 miles distant!* Torreya is a RARE TREE found only in this park. GREGORY HOUSE is an 1849 *cotton plantation home* which prospered during "steamboating days". GUIDED TOURS are weekdays 11 a.m. and 2 p.m.; Sat. and Sun. hourly from 9 a.m. to 4 p.m. On a scale of 1 to 10 this park rates 15!!! Be sure to *explore for* *blackberries* (both sides of road) on entrance drive to park, late May and June. I picked enough for a pie!

Bristol, FL, North on Rd. 12 — *(850) 643-2674*
Open Daily, 8 a.m.-Sunset — *Admission Fee*

AN AERIAL EXPERIENCE

Enter with "curiosity". Exit in "wonderment". **NATIONAL MUSEUM OF NAVAL AVIATION** is 1 of 3 *federally-sanctioned aviation museums* — Other 2 are Smithsonian's National Air & Space Museum in D.C. and U.S. Air Force Museum in Ohio!! So much for prestige . . . here are the facts. Exhibit space — 250,000 square feet. Over **50 aircraft** including a Desert Storm jet (A-7E Corsair II) which dropped bombs on Iraq. Site is 37 wooded acres (picnic tables) on Pensacola Bay. **WEST WING** contains *4-story complex* of aircraft carrier technology with carrier island structure and wooden flight deck. **BLUE ANGEL ATRIUM** is *7 stories* connecting east and west wings with 4 Blue Angel Skyhawks suspended in diamond formation. Note aircraft nicknames: Truculent Turtle; Banshee Liftmaster; Bearcat; Avenger; Helldiver and many more! Browse through yourself or *take the tour* daily at 9:30 and 11 a.m. or 1 and 2:30 p.m. Special tours call (904) 452-9304.

Pensacola, FL, Naval Air Station — *(850) 452-3606*
Open Daily, 9-5. Closed Christmas, Thanksgiving, New Years
Admission FREE

SEVILLE HISTORIC DISTRICT

A **25-block area** much like *New Orleans* with Creole heritage dating to 1559. The west side boundary is Tarragona St. where oldtime trolley tracks remain. 1832 CHRIST CHURCH is now a museum. Streets and side alleys are laced with **Creole style homes.** One such is *Julee Cottage* 1805 owned by a succession of "free women of color", now a Black History Museum. **Seville Square,** a lovely *green lawn plaza* is focal point of the area — unusual shops and food purveyors ring the plaza. Do explore MUSEUM OF INDUSTRY and MUSEUM OF COMMERCE ON Zaragoza St. "Shotgun Homes" are intriguing as is **ST. MICHAELS CEMETERY** with its *raised brick "oven" tombs* similar to New Orleans famed cemeteries. If time allows, amble down to the Bayfront to Pitts Slip Marina . . . Boats are always exciting!!!

Pensacola, FL, Downtown, Near Hwy. 98 — *Info: 1-800-343-4321*
Historic District Open Daily — *Admission FREE*
Museums Open Mon. through Sat. 10-4 — *(850) 444-8905*
Admission Fee

FLORIDA'S SWEETEST PLACE

Chipola River's natural overflow created a vast swamp which is home to white **TUPELO GUM TREES.** For 125 years *beekeepers in the* *river valley* have produced a delectable "honey" which never crystallizes (goes to sugar). Trees blossom in **MAY** and the honey is shipped worldwide. Area around **WEWAHITCHKA** makes Florida the 3rd largest honey producer in the nation!! Town name is a jawbreaker so locals call it "WEWA". Wewahitchka is Indian for water eyes . . . on the edge of town are two oblong lakes that resemble a perfect pair of eyes. Wewa is famous also for its **DEAD LAKES STATE RECREATION AREA.** Here are 83 acres overlooking 2 dead lakes chock full of *cypress, oaks and pines* drowned by river overflows. Fishermen come from hundreds of miles to angle in the dead lakes. I observed plenty of bass and perch catches and the b-i-g-g-e-s-t carp near the dam I've ever seen!! Unbelievable *tree forms* provide fine camera shots. **CAMPING** is on a shady hillside blanketed with soft wiregrass. Town has crystallized plans for an annual HONEY FESTIVAL in April. South of Wewa on Rd. 71 are "Honeyville" and "Gaskins Still" . . . guess what they produce???

Wewahitchka, FL, Rd. 71, Dead Lakes Rec. Area *(850) 639-2702*
Open Daily, 8-Sunset *Admission Fee*

BRADLEY'S COUNTRY STORE 1927

If you've got a great product, the world will beat a path to your door!! So it is with the **BLUE RIBBON SAUSAGE** that Grandma Mary Bradley began casing in 1910 . . . Few businesses boast *a 70-year track record!!* The modest store is rustic surrounded by a pond, pines and bearded oaks — you have to slow up for the curve so you may as well visit. The **smokehouse aroma** is irresistible — get your wallet out! Sales average 65,000 pounds yearly. Choose from *specially seasoned sausage, hogshead cheese, liver pudding, cracklings, milled grits or Ozark cured hams.* Customers range from governors to humble folk and a mailing list from Pacific to the Atlantic. Do stop by. Bradley's is on the **NATIONAL REGISTER OF HISTORIC PLACES.**

Tallahassee, FL, 12 mi. N.E. on Hwy. 151, Centerville Rd. *(850) 893-1647*
Open Mon. thru Sat. 8-6; Closed Sun. *Admission FREE*

CARLSBAD EAST — FLORIDA CAVERNS

Our caves may be smaller but for *stunning forms* and *beauty* they rank right up there with the other 2 U.S. cave systems . . . and like the others they even have **bats!** In fact they consume 900 pounds of insects nightly. Formations of *soda straws, draperies, columns, stalactites and flowstone* astound visitors to the honeycomb of connecting rooms in this cave system. *Underground trails* twist and turn beneath 1,783 acres beside the **CHIPOLA RIVER.** Daily TOURS take one hour and leave every half hour from 9 a.m. to 5 p.m. **BLUE HOLE** is a frigid swim spring near the 32-site CAMP AREA! Great spot to cool down your watermelons! An *extensive trail* meanders along the river plain. CANOES and SMALL BOATS are tailor-made for the CHIPOLA RIVER because of its narrow winding character. Surprise!! Visiting is

not expensive as the caverns are part of the FLORIDA PARK SYSTEM!!!

Marianna, FL, SR 167 *(850) 482-9598*
Open Daily, 8 a.m.-Sunset *Admission Fee*

DESTIN DOCKS — JETTIES

Mile-long **Destin Harbor** was the site for the pioneer snapper fishing industry in late 1800's. Hundreds of boats (fleets, charters, private craft) still bring the big ones in. **DOCKS** are exciting 'cause you can see the iced-down catches up close — they sell, you buy! Lots of *eateries on pilings line the wharf* and have marvelous water views. A long, dazzling white sand bar hems the harbor on its south side. West of the harbor a pair of huge **rock jetties** and an emerald ribbon of water lead to the Gulf. Clear saltwater jetties are *favorite hangouts for divers* searching for fish and artifacts!!! If you want scenic shots and are curious about what "hook-n-liners" are getting, stroll DESTIN BRIDGE CATWALK on south side of East Pass Bridge. It is 3,000 feet! Near the DOCKS you will find parking but in some strange places (little back alleys and side streets)! Across the bridge (southwest side) are dunes and sand bars that don't quit, part of **Eglin Air Force Base!** The whole area and CHOCTAWHATCHEE BAY is mega-scenic!!!

Destin, FL, southeast side of East Pass Bridge
Open Daily *Admission FREE*

NAVAL LIVE OAKS

This tough **Live Oak Forest** was purchased in 1828 by the U.S. government. Much of the 1,378 acres is covered by heavy oaks (a cubic foot can weigh 75 lbs.). They were used in shipbuilding as early as 1700 because oak resists decay and grows to 50 feet high!! The ship, CONSTITUTION, ("old ironsides") was made of live oak . . . Before this was a **national park,** I would sail into Butcherpen Cove, climb the high cliffs and marvel at the majestic forest growing atop this steep land ridge. Today visitors walk a short path from the parking lot to view moss-draped "senator oaks" and the *panorama of PENSACOLA BAY!!!* Visitors Center contains **excellent displays.** A ¾ mile *nature stroll* leads to an *overlook* on Santa Rosa Sound — picnic here too. Naval Live Oaks was young America's first timber preserve with an original tract of 30,000 acres. Area now extends over 2 miles long on both sides on Hwy. 98.

East of Gulf Breeze, FL, on Santa Rosa Island, U.S. 98
(850) 934-2600 or 934-2635 or 932-5302
Open Daily, 8:30-5 *Admission FREE*

HIGH POINT-LOW POINT (SHELL POINT)

State high point is 345 foot Britton Hill in LAKEWOOD, Walton County. Sawmills made floors for Waldorf Astoria & Grand Central Station. 17 acre park straddles the would-be-mountain. Short trails lead to vista overlook with distant views for (10 miles)! ! ! Off Rd 285 low point (sea level) is a tiny sea-side village of SHELL POINT, Wakulla County. Countless sailboats snug-up to maze of canals & basin. OLD SEAFARER'S CHAPEL guards white cove swim beach overlooking small offshore "islets". Plan-a-stay at Shell Pt Resort---made to order Gulf "sunsets" & a delicious eatery! ! ! Explore LIVE OAK ISLAND & Spring Creek. Off Rd 365.

Shell Point Resort, Shell Point, FL *1-800-926-7163 or (904) 926-7163*

ANTIQUE CAR MUSEUM

Rare collection numbers (70) & includes LINCOLN's Horse Drawn Hearse, 1913 Car-Nation (1 of 3) in world, 1948 Tucker (one from the movie) and 1931 Duesenberg ($1,000,000). A quite old knife exhibit can be admired also.

Tallahassee, FL 3550 A Hwy 90 East *(850) 942-0137*
Open Mon-Sat 10-6, Sun Noon-6 *Admission Fee*

ARCADIA MILL ARCHEOLOGICAL SITE

Arcadia Mill was a water-powered industrial complex on Pond Creek. It included a stone quarry, sawmill, gristmill, bucket factory, cotton textile mill and the second oldest Florida railroad. J. Forsyth began his venture in 1828. When sawmill operations moved to Bagdad the Arcadia site was devoted to a textile factory by 1845. Ten years later the mill burned and **1990 excavations** found the burned artifacts on the mill floor to be in good condition! The long *80-foot dam* is being reconstructed and **Ironstone** is visible along the site which is still being dug out at various levels. *A suspension foot bridge* swings over the swift moving creek. The 30-acre site is heavily wooded and Arcadia House on grounds combines as a lab residence and information center for visitors. This new exciting archeological site is being restored as monies are available — you'll be impressed with what has been done in so short a time!!

Milton, FL, Hwy. 90 (north side), west of P.J.C. Campus. Go north on Mill Pond Lane, west on Anna Simpson Rd. and north on Timothy Twitchell Drive.
Open Daily *C of C (850) 623-2339*
FREE

LEON SINKS

Sinks form when underground rock and soil layers erode, often taking millions of years. These deep depressions can be WET SINKS or DRY SINKS. **LEON SINKS GEOLOGICAL AREA** is 548 acres of **rare**

land forms, vegetation and **wildlife.** Part of the tract is developed with *boardwalks, foot bridges,* and *interpretive trails.* Paths cross Fisher Creek's wild azaleas, Sink (rock faces), Lost Stream which disappears in dry season and Natural Bridge, a land "walkover" between 2 sinks. **BIG DISMAL SINK** is a deep steep *wet sink* with endangered plant communities . . . the sound of running water is heard from view platform. Near *Bear Scratch Trail* are Yucca plants (bear grass), so called as they are used to prepare bear meat during curing process. **SULLIVAN SINK** was the site in 1988 where *highly professional cave divers* entered to swim 1½ miles downstream (often 200 feet deep) to Cheryl Sink in Waculla County. About **5 miles of trails** exist. Observation platforms and interpretive signs are well placed. Other sinks names are: Black, Big Eight, No Name, Magnolia and others. Leon Sinks is a new "natural site" only opened in 1990's . . . Bet before the year 2000 it will be a Visitor Hot Spot!!! (MAP Pg. 57)

Tallahassee, FL, 9 mi. south off Hwy. 319
Wakulla Ranger District (850) 926-3561
Open Daily — *Admission FREE*

MILLION DOLLAR PLAYGROUND

Most folks don't realize that they can use **EGLIN AIR FORCE BASE OUTDOOR RECREATION AREA** which extends over hundreds of thousands of acres! Off Rd. 285 is **BLUE SPRINGS,** a lovely freshwater swim picnic spot, or off SR 85 is popular **TURKEY CREEK,** family fun place. I've logged *hundreds of miles* taking my house guests (scenic touring) through green cathedral forest roads . . . Terrain is never the same. Always surprises over the next hill. *CAMPING AREAS* number 16, often overlooking ponds and creeks. The **Yellow** and **Shoal Rivers** attract boaters and run for miles through the reservation. Aromatic white blossom titi forests are everywhere and countless *branches* and *creeks* crosshatch Eglin . . . Some more colorful "handles" are Lost Boy Creek, Boiling Creek, Pocosin Pond, Gin Hole Landing and Rogue Crick! The following is a partial list of the many activities for Eglin visitors: Canoeing, Fishing, Bicycling, Hiking, Hunting, Horseback Riding and Pleasure Driving. Off Rd. 20 (near Pipin Lake) is **WHITE POINT,** a popular swim beach on *Choctawhatchee Bay* . . . Do purchase a map (small fee) at Jackson Guard.

Niceville, FL, SR 85 — *(850) 882-4164*
JACKSON GUARD Hours Mon.-Fri., 7-3:15
OUTDOOR REC. AREA Open Daily
Permits required at above address or write: Jackson Guard, 107 Crestview Ave., Niceville, FL 32578 — *Admission By Permit*

Scenic Drives

PECAN PLANTATION ROAD

North of "historic" Monticello lies green **hill country** (some over 300 feet)!! Long years ago manored southern families all kept private *pecan orchards.* Many still remain, adding elegance to the drive . . . I took the path in **APRIL** so every growing thing was "busting its bloomers" in fine style. Blankets of red clover mix with blue spiderworts to line the roadside. Dignified farm homes with neat outbuildings crown some hills while others nest in lowland hollows. At **NEW HOPE GROCERY** there is a *wee park* with rock fireplaces and the most **GRANDIOSE OAKS** I've ever seen . . . Adjoining this park (north side) is a country lane (unpaved) straight out of TARA HALL, remember G.W.T.W.??? A freeness settles 'round the traveler out here (no fences)!! Look for **WHITE FRINGE TREES** along this *sometimes canopied* **14-MILE DRIVE.** Its unusual blooms resemble a lacy beard. If you want a DETOUR take Grooverville Road — bet it's Groovy!!!

Monticello, FL, Take Hwy. 19-57 north for 14 miles
Open Daily *Admission Free*

RIVERS —N— WOODS

Start point is off Rd. 20, go south on Rd. 375 (Smith Creek Rd.) Road is paved and skirts the east side of **OCHLOCKONEE RIVER.** Soapstone Branch is one of many creeks, branches and small streams crosshatching the area . . . A short distance and you enter **APALACHICOLA NATIONAL FOREST** where April wildflowers, pinks, yellows, whites, crimsons, all jumble together crowding the roadsides!! *Family cemeteries* are not unusual — **Thomas Burial Plot** with picket fence adds history and charm to the drive . . . A nearby grocery store shares ground with the family cemetery where the former owner was buried according to his wishes facing his beloved country store! Postcard-pretty farmhouses dot the landscape. I detoured to Porter Lake, going west on Rd. 13 (paved). Go 2.9 miles to enjoy a small camp area (6 sites), picnic facilities, grills and small landing on **Ochlockonee River** — *Hickory and Tulip Poplars* are gorgeous! Forest roads are well marked (some are lumpier than others). Drive ends 25 miles south at **SOPCHOPPY,** out of the hi-rent district. Here you may buy 2 hot dogs for 89ᶜ while you figure out "how to get home"!!!

20 miles west of Tallahassee, FL, Directions above

BACK BAY BAYOU COUNTRY

At Greenpoint take Rd. 65 north. **Bear Creek** and **Cash Bayou** begin a *series of back bays ringed by young cypress.* Loblolly bays with mini-magnolia blooms are everywhere. Whiskey George Creek looked like a "heavy-duty fish hole"! At bridge over *Doyle Creek* is a small boat put-in and the northeast side is a pretty spot for a blanket picnic waterside. The first **7 miles** of the drive, thick carpets of pink sabatia, meadow beauties, yellow spikes and blue spiderworts created a roadside rainbow! Ft. Gadsden Creek is one of many streams draining **TATES HELL SWAMP** . . . I detoured north on Rd. 379 to tiny **SUMATRA,** a farm-town, once famed for its tobacco! A post office, cemetery and busy general store still remain. Country folk don't lack imagination in naming their surroundings — I passed Chiggerville Lane, Hoecake Road and the Slip and Slide Bar!!! North section of this 30-mile scenic path becomes more hilly and do circle LAKE MYSTIC *(deep turquoise lake)* on Rd. 12. Your lovely ride ends at Bristol where I found friendly "down home ca-juns" serving *Louisiana Bodouin Sausage* at the local pit barbecue!!!

Greenpoint, FL, 10 mi. east of Apalachicola, Rd. 65
Open Daily *Admission FREE*

BAY BLUFFS SCENIC HIGHWAY

This hilly **10-mile** ribbon of road was built in 1927 on *steep red clay cliffs* overlooking 3 bays (Pensacola, Escambia and East Bay). **Bricks** from these bluffs are in the walls of *Fort Pickens, Fort Barrancas and Pensacola Lighthouse.* I began my ride on the south end near Bayou Tex-ar (Tay-har). Within a few miles look for a cemetery on the west road-side. Directly to the east is a **wooden overlook** and "walk-down". A few hundred feet north is **Bay Bluff Scenic Park** with steps all-the-way-down-bay-bluffs to water's edge (if you've the knees . . . I faded on this one)! Further north is an old vine-covered *chimney,* all that remains of Hyer Knowles steam sawmill built in 1857. Recent years have seen a property demand to build homes along the panoramic highway and so a preserva-tion group for SCENIC HIGHWAY has been formed. Several vantage points along the route offer spectacular views. Drive can originate from the north via Hwy. 90 or I-10.

Pensacola, FL, Hwy 90 (west side Pensacola Bay)
Open Daily *Admission FREE*

COTTON RIDGE

North of Milton, FL, country Rd. 87 rolls through **ridgeland** blanketed with **COTTON FARMS.** Santa Rosa is the only county in Florida with a *"Cotton Gin".* A blue mist hangs atop some ridges in ear-ly morning. Some slopes are *high enough* to see several miles in the distance. Nearby is **BIG COLDWATER CREEK** where canoeing and tubing are "big" leisure activities. In April, snow-white Dogwood were poking their noses almost into the roadway. Along the 15-mile drive much acreage is devoted to **PECAN GROVES.** In *November* some farms allow you the pleasure of gathering the nuts yourself (they always taste better)!! Summer brings veggie stands selling greens, collards and the best corn I ever tasted. I passed unusual businesses . . . cricket farms, a beagle hunting pup sale ($35)! Drive dead-ends on Hwy. 4. Go west and you hit town of JAY (Texas East), a 1970 *oil boom town* . . . you can tell who struck it rich by the "Christmas Trees" in their yards or farm fields (these are the piping and small pumps still bringing up black gold). Go east on Rd. 4 and you hit town of Berrydale on fringes of BLACKWATER STATE FOREST (supercalifragilistic woodlands)!!!

Milton, FL, Hwy. 87
Open Daily *Admission FREE*

Unique Shopping

HAVANA U.S.A.

In 1829 the town flourished growing Cuban tobacco. Since 1984 Havana cultivates **Antique "buffs and pros"!!** One ole timey shop has now multiplied to **11 antique stores. SATURDAY AND SUNDAY** are busiest for poking about. Some shops specialize in *Oak Furniture, Brass, Kitchenware and Decorative Glass* — my "thing" was the bric-a-brac and doo-dad counters. Most dealers are located on **N. Main St.** or **7th St.** and proprietors love to banter or trade antique stories with visitors. It seems appropriate that in modern times Havana takes on an *historical perspective* since it was the site in mid 1600's of the SPANISH MISSION of SANTA CRUZ De CUPALI!! By 1998 antique district ballooned to 8 blocks!!

Havana, FL, Hwy. 27-63 (10 mi. northwest of Tallahassee)
Open Daily

1/2 OFF TICKETED PRICE

First you have to find GRACEVILLE. It's in Florida (barely) 2 miles from Alabama line. What draws **MILLIONS OF VISITORS** annually to a town with a population of 2200??? *SHOPPING,* of course! **VF FACTORY OUTLET** runs the most gargantuan retail trading center I've ever visited. Mammoth brick building has *2 sections.* One is devoted to clothing, lingerie, swim and sportswear. The names are there . . . Vanity Fair; Jantzen, Lee, Lollipop; Basset-Walker! The *2nd outlet area* sells Corning-Revere Ware; Black & Decker; Bass and Banister shoes; Luggage; Evan Picone men's wear; Van Heusen; Jewelry and Cosmetics and on-and-on-and-on!!! Other outlet centers have sprung up to ride the coattail success of VF's booming business. They add competition and selection. License plates in parking lots read: Tallahassee-Orlando-Atlanta-Pensacola-Mobile-Key West "ad infinitum". As I roamed VF Factory Outlet I took advantage of the *½ off ticket prices* buying jog suits, lingerie, perfume and (natch) JEWELRY. My 2-hour visit was not sufficient to shop even 50% of the outlet stores so get an early start!! If you don't tire and still have a full wallet, drive to **BOAZ, ALABAMA.** I'm told there is a retail outlet center 4 times bigger than Graceville's . . . Holy Cow . . . !

Graceville, FL, Hwy. 77 (15 mi. northwest of Marianna) (850) 263-3207
Open Daily Mon.-Thurs., 9-6; Fri, 9-8; Sun., 12:30-5:30 Admission FREE

Bubbling Springs

PONCE DE LEON SPRINGS

2ND MAGNITUDE 68° FLOW 14 MILLION GALLONS DAILY

This is a **STATE RECREATION AREA** used for *swimming and sunning.* "Boils" bubble up from 3 vents where 19 feet below are underground caverns. The run flows to Choctawhatchee River. Activities are nature trails and fishing. Park acreage is 443 acres **(very scenic).** Try exploring the town of *Ponce de Leon* (won't take long) and *Red Bay* — City Slickers won't see much but I think these backwoods hamlets are unique — they are the "backbone" of AMERICA!!

Ponce de Leon, FL, West of Bonifay, FL, Off Hwy. 90,
Rd. 181 NO DIVING (850) 836-4281
Open Daily, 8-Sunset Admission Fee

GINNIE SPRINGS

2ND MAGNITUDE 72° FLOW 29 MILLION GALLONS DAILY

I don't think guests here ever sleep! So many activities — *Swim, Snorkel, Tube, Canoe, DIVE, Underwater Photography.* Plenty of elbow room in the **200-acre wooded park. SIX SPRINGS** on property have gin-clear visibility . . . Devil's Eye was my favorite. Popular is a *2-mile tube "drift"* on SANTE FE RIVER. Here is wilderness camping along a 2-mile riverfront. Tent. RV's full hook-up. Ginnie is a complete Dive Resort having a large dive scuba store, country store and pantry. Whatever is needed, you'll get (rentals, instruction, refills)! This is one of America's **premier dive sites** with visitors from all over the world. Submerged swaying eelgrass creates graceful dances. Extensive **CAVE SYSTEMS** lie beneath limestone ledges . . . "Come on down", literally!!!

High Springs, FL, Rd. 340 (904) 454-2202
Out of Florida, 800-874-8571
Open Daily Admission Fee

BLUE SPRING

1ST MAGNITUDE 70° FLOW 186 MILLION GALLONS DAILY

This has been the **local swimming hole** for generations of Marianna folks. An extensive high hill on spring's north side shows complete *total beauty* of the spot. **THREE** main vents boil up to create what is called *Merritts Mill Pond.* Blue-green clear water is circled by giant shadowy cypress swamp. Pond is **4 miles long,** bordered by numerous springs and sinks! Hillside picnic and food concessions open in summertime. Blue Springs is a swimming park operated by city of Marianna. NO diving is allowed.

Marianna, FL (5 mi. east) on Rd. 164
Open Summertime *Admission Fee*

CYPRESS SPRINGS

1ST MAGNITUDE 72° FLOW 90 MILLION GALLONS DAILY

A **NEW DIVE SITE** explored in 1985. Pool is circular with 150-foot diameter, surrounded by green cypress. A *cave* extends to 70 feet deep opening to a room 40 by 14 feet high. A 1,000-foot "run" discharges into Holmes Creek. Non-divers enjoy a **3-mile tubing trip.** Dogwood trees are sprinkled about the 6-acre hardwood **CAMPING AREA.** *Canoe rentals* are available. Cypress Springs has some of the world's *clearest water* (300 foot visibility)!! Great variety of plants and fish.

Vernon, FL, 2 mi. north Hwy. 79 *(850) 535-2960*
Open Daily *Admission Fee*

BRANFORD SPRINGS

2ND MAGNITUDE 73° FLOW 19 MILLION GALLONS DAILY

Shallow spring site used mainly for swimming and snorkeling — then how come great numbers of *serious divers* frequent the spot??? **BRANFORD DIVE CENTER** is on the grounds, that's why! Spring is ideal for checking out new equipment and instruction. B.D.C. caters to the dive crowd and the store has every type gidgit for underwater use. A *new service* which has *"caught on"* is the **Boat Charter, Shuttle** and **Night Dive** programs. Half or full day trips (complete with cook-outs) are available . . . to TROY, ROYAL, LITTLE RIVER, ROCK BLUFF, PEACOCK and many other springs. Branford consists of 2 pools (85 ft. and 65 ft. wide). Wooden decking surrounds the 9-foot-deep spring. This boil peeks down on the mighty **SUWANNEE RIVER!**

Branford, FL *Bradford Dive Center (904) 935-1141*
Juncture of Hwy. 27 and Hwy. 129 (Southeast Side of Bridge)
Open Daily *Admission FREE*

VORTEX SPRING

2ND MAGNITUDE 68° FLOW 25 MILLION GALLONS DAILY

Located on **360 acres of hillcountry.** Basin is 250 feet wide by 50 feet deep. Caverns descend to 115 feet beside stunning limestone rock features. A *permanent handrail* allows divers a leisurely exploration. Curious fish (13 species) shadow divers. **BLUE CREEK RUN** (4 miles) resembles a *glass bottom boat ride* . . . canoeists and snorkelers love it. Groups use the Lodge for *overnights* and Otter Creek Lodge has kitchenettes. There is a super-duper barbeque pit for big groups. The resort has **horseback riding trail,** *hike paths* and *All Terrain Vehicle* riding. I'm plumb "tuckered out" reading about all this activity. Camp/dive store has latest fandango dive equipment (rent or buy)!! **Spring Restaurant** handles *yummy breakfasts* and short order food . . . Almost forgot, bring your rig. There's **CAMPING!**

Ponce De Leon, FL, 4 mi. north off Hwy. 81 *(850) 836-4979*
Open Daily *Admission Fee*

MORRISON SPRING

2ND MAGNITUDE 76° FLOW 40 MILLION GALLONS DAILY

A 250-foot pool bordered by swamp forest. Said to have excellent **ledge diving.** Caverns open to a spacious room with depths to 90 feet. Location is *remote* and you will **avoid crowds** at Morrison . . . A dive concession operates rentals, air and snack bar. Swimming, fishing and snorkeling are allowed.

Red Bay, FL, 5 mi. northeast off Hwy. 81 *(850) 836-4223*
Open Daily *Admission Fee*

Animal Places

FIFTY-FIVE ACRES OF LEARNING

Florida *"beasties"*, panther, red wolf and other critters, roam in a natural setting at **TALLAHASSEE JUNIOR MUSEUM.** Over 100,000 folks visit the **Habitat Zoo** yearly. A **Boardwalk Nature Trail** winds about a wet and dry woods environment. Highlight for me was the diverse historic buildings on grounds . . . an 1880's **Big Bend Farm Complex** and **BELLEVUE,** *antebellum plantation home* of Prince Murat.

Don't be bashful if you're not toting "little folk" . . . This is a standout "Alfresco" museum!!

Tallahassee, FL, off Lake Bradford Rd. *(850) 575-8684 or 576-1636*
Near Airport, 3945 Museum Dr.
Open Tues.-Sun., Closed Mon. *Admission Fee*

THE ZOO

There are 50 acres, 600 animals, 200,000 visitors a year and a *hustle-bustle* staff of 50!! In the "Walk Through Area" (20 acres) the main attraction is **gorilla habitat** where COLOSSUS, a male silverback and MUKE, a 26-year-old female, are being encouraged to produce a little "COLUKE"! All 5 ape species are represented at The Zoo . . . I'm partial to the gentle Orangs. Much money and care went into the *design* of these habitats where viewing is from both lower and elevated vantage points. A **productive breeding program** appears right on target and Director Quinn notes that nutrition is an important component. Groceries run into thousands of dollars (daily)! Kids get to *feed giraffe,* take **ELEPHANT RIDES** or enjoy the barnyard exhibit . . . Wait, there's more . . . **A TRAINRIDE** takes visitors through 30 acres *where 150 animals roam free.* In 1991 WHITE TIGERS came to live at the Zoo! **Exotic Botanicals** on grounds create a "garden atmosphere". A (people) food emporium serves up goodies. Out of 1400 licensed zoos and aquariums in the U.S. THE ZOO is one of the *rare 140 which are accredited!!!*

Gulf Breeze, FL, 5701 Gulfbreeze Pkwy., *(850) 932-2229*
Hwy. 98, 8 mi. east of Gulf Breeze
Open Daily. Winter, 9-4; Summer, 9-5.
Closed Thanksgiving & Christmas *Admission Fee*

LOVE, TOUCH, PET, HAND-FEED

A rather large task when you have 220 animals (47 species) from 34 countries! Owners say this is their prescription for success and they love, touch, pet and hand-feed on a *daily basis!!* Result is "happy animals". The **SASQUATCH COUNTRY PARK** is 48 acres covered by a green umbrella of Post Oak, Black Oak and Red Oak. Paths wind through 10 acres of animal compound with the rest being grazeland for brood stock. There are antelope, deer, ostrich and many other hoofed animals who after a day of entertaining children love being turned loose in the pastures!! There are **3 mountain lions.** *Largest cougar weighs 265 pounds.* Cats eat 6½ pounds of red meat and chicken daily. All creatures have names and respond to them. Curious George, a ground ape, is a natural clown; Paucha is a friendly llama; Micah (mountain lion) is a real "ham" and *comes running over to greet visitors!!!* Streamlined Mack is a 26-inch miniature horse, and Pandora is a 7½ foot boa petted by thousands of kids. There are **hundreds** more critters to meet and study in this CLEANEST of CLEAN zoos . . . It costs $285 a day for food and preventive medicine at Sasquatch. Animals receive *childlike care* and before they are put to bed each evening owners "tuck them in" with popcorn, peanuts and bedtime snacks!!! I was much impressed by SASQUATCH and its animal tenders.

Crestview, FL (3 mi. east) US 90 — *(850) 682-3949*
Open Mon.-Fri., 11-4; Sat.-Sun., 9-5:30 — *Admission Fee*

GULFARIUM

Highlight of the visit is the **LIVING SEA** which is a natural setting with clear glass windows for viewing and *photographing* shark, stingrays, **giant sea turtles,** eel and strange deep sea species. There are shows with loveable, huggable porpoise performing split-second-timing tricks. Sea lions (born clowns) also do shows. Other exhibits and shows include tropical *penguin, otters, harbor seals,* and *alligators!* Show times: May to September, 10 a.m., noon, 2 p.m., 4 p.m., and 6 p.m.; October to April, 10 a.m., noon, 2 p.m., and 4 p.m.

Fort Walton Beach, FL, Hwy. 98 E. — *(850) 244-5169*
Open Daily — *Admission Fee*

GULF WORLD

Stroll *tropical gardens* where continuous running shows include sea lion, porpoises, parrots and scuba show displays. **Penguin Island** is an unusual habitat of these comic-looking sea creatures.

Panama City Beach, FL, 15412 W. Hwy. 98A — *(850) 234-5271*
Open Daily — *Admission Fee*

Lake Seminole

A 500-MILE LAKESHORE

W-A-Y bigger than Lake Okeechobee is **LAKE SEMINOLE** (but it's man-made) . . . you know Who made the other one! In 1950's the Corps of Engineers built **Jim Woodruff Lock and Dam** to create a "pool" of 37,500 acres. About 50% of the lake's **500-mile shoreline** lies in the "Sunshine State". *Recreational facilities* in Florida number about 20 and many are in the "5 Diamond Category"! Most nestle on *STEEP BLUFFS* overlooking the sometimes gentle, sometimes wild, lake waters. Rimming the lake are **deep forests** where I've viewed deer casually emerge, crossing to a corn field! The Corps of Engineers spends millions of dollars on many *outstanding public recreational facilities* ringing the lake. The following articles will detail several of these spots which I consider v-e-r-y s-p-e-c-i-a-l! (MAP Pg. 54)

Chattahoochee, FL, Hwy. 90 *Open Daily*

NEALS LANDING

The 3 things making this site superb are: location, location, location! It nestles on the west bank of **Apalachicola River.** Towering trees and a mix of wildflowers combine with a *remote spot* to create a wonderful outdoor haven. A boat ramp provides river access for water-skiing or fishing. Tent and trailer camping (self-contained) is roomy. Grills, bathhouses, rest rooms, complete the facilities . . . Another nearby fun spot for investigation is **BUENA VISTA LANDING.** There are stabilized sites for rigs to camp, a boat ramp, DEEP WOODS and lots of redbirds!

Chattahoochee, FL (15 mi. northwest). Just east of juncture of Hwy. 2 and Rd. 271 *(912) 662-2001*
Open Daily *Admission; Day Use FREE*

UPTOWN COUNTRY COOKING

You'll discover a 20-year tradition (still on the front burner) at **PARRAMORE LANDING RESTAURANT.** Hillside eatery has a scenic view of Apalachicola backwaters. Folks come for the food . . . catfish, crab, shrimp, oysters — if it swims, they serve it! The landing is a *serious fisherman's hideout.* It's just like a magnet, attracting anglers and diners from as far as Canada. Baitroom opens at 6 a.m. **CAMPING** is possible (full hook-ups), a bit crowded. (Sheltered) boat slips are rented. A *day picnic area* is a good spot to watch all the "goings-on" at the landing. If you're not going to picnic or fish then you only need to bring one thing . . . A Hearty Appetite!!

Sneads, FL, (10 mi. northwest), off Rd. 271 *(850) 592-2091*
Park Open Daily *Admission FREE*
Restaurant Open Tues.-Fri., 4-9; Sat. & Sun. 11-10.
Closed Monday *(850) 592-2091*
Admission FREE

DRIVE-THRU WATERGARDEN

During the 1950's backup water from the Woodruff Dam created a series of interconnecting *lagoons, bayous, marshes, ponds and lakes.* A paved road (Rd. 271) straddles an *8-mile stretch* of this lovely **Natural Botanical Marsh Garden!!!** Fragile white swamp lilies bloom in profusion. Views are of tall Cypress, white blossomed Loblolly Bays and Willows. Graceful long-necked water birds quietly feed in the shallows and I spotted about 6 varieties of duck. *Roadside pull-offs* are everywhere with much shade and privacy. Islands are visible and to the east are grand vistas of 37,000-acre Lake Seminole. Backwater inlets have wildflower displays like white and yellow pitcher plants, grass pinks, purple drum heads and the pink marshmallow. All of this beauty is part of APALACHEE WILDLIFE MANAGEMENT AREA (7,952 acres). Boat Access is the ideal way to enjoy the complete refuge . . . however, there is a **WALK-IN PATH** near *T.J. Road* close to the check station gate. Walk-in area is open all year (except hunt season). Info: (904) 265-3676. Primitive **CAMPING** is allowed. Both water and uplands are remote . . . this accounts for healthy populations of beaver, coyote, fox, mink, otter, bobcat and deer. I am an amateur photographer and discovered endless "snapping opportunities". Don't miss this "unusual drive tour" . . . Mother Nature awaits! (MAP Pg. 63)

Sneads, FL, (3 mi. north), Rd. 271 — *Apalachee W.M.A. (850) 265-3676*
Open Daily — *Admission FREE*

THREE RIVERS STATE PARK

Here are the facts: Named for nearby **Flint, Chattahoochee** and **Apalachicola Rivers.**

Acres 834
Shoreline . . . . 4 miles
Terrain . . . . Hilly Bluffs
Camping . . . . *By Lakeside*
Location . . . . Remote
Rec. Facilities . . . . Boat Ramp, Picnic Shelters, Day Use Area
Activities . . . . . Fish Dock, *Scenic Overlook,* (2) Hike Trails.
Animal Life . . . deer, grey fox, many "gators"; Fine bird watching.
General Description . . . . On 37,500-acre Lake Seminole, heavy wooded Scenic area.

Three Rivers State Recreation Area, *Sneads, FL, Rd. 271* — *(850) 482-9006*
Open Daily, 8-Sunset — *Admission Fee*

WEST OVERLOOK SNEADS LANDING

Late in 1880's Sneads, a pioneer dentist, landed here probably greeted by scads of alligators. Today visitors are welcomed by a full-blown resort. Corps of Engineers operates a quite **beachy swimming park** on Lake Seminole's south shore. There's enough velvet green grass to play golf!! Horseshoe pits, playground, waterside lunch facilities, make for year-round fun. Another section of the million dollar project is **SEMINOLE LODGE** and **MARINA.** Motel is on a quiet bayou and several houseboats were bobbing at anchor during my visit. Lake Seminole has about 250 odd-sized **Islands** mostly in the northern region. Boat rentals, snack and groceries concession, on grounds . . . CAMPING is popular. A "must see" is **WEST OVERLOOK** at Woodruff Dam where a panorama of mighty dam controls, rolling hills and a "no end" shoreline create stunning views. (MAP Pg. 54)

Sneads, FL, Hwy. 90 — *Corps Resource Office (912) 662-2814*
Seminole Lodge (850) 593-6886
Open Daily — *Day Use and Swim Park Admission FREE*

ALMOST MOUNTAINS AND CANADIAN GEESE

Roads (all paved) are so s-t-e-e-p I used low gear. Entrance to **EAST BANK CAMPGROUND** and **DAY USE AREA** should be named *"Rollercoaster Lane"*. Whole area is crosshatched with ravines, hollows, and valleys, many terminating in natural amphitheaters!! Corps of Engineers run East Bank Recreation facilities and they are the *"Creme de la Creme"!* Campsites (69) overlook Lake Seminole with view of islands and stone bluffs . . . There are tennis courts, overlooks, horseshoe pits, lunch verandas under moss-draped Oaks. I admired scores of graceful long-necked **Canadian Geese** paddling round. About 50 of them are *permanent residents* on Ol' Sem and their honking is heard for some distance. They are big fellers and each year turn out a healthy crop of "young-uns". Swimming and sunbathing are big at East Bank. Stroll along TURKEY FLIGHT nature trail and overlook. Woods critters here include squirrels that look more like *teddy bears* with whiteish ears. Do see **RIVER JUNCTION ACCESS** — mighty fancy boat docks, ramps, boardwalks, sheltered tie-up slips on a quiet canal. If you're a history buff, check out **White Cemetery** (modest brick entrance) on the main road in. Tour on up to HUTCHINSON'S FERRY LANDING . . . Wingate's restaurant will set your mouth watering!!! (MAP Pg. 54)

East Bank Public Use Area *East Bank Campground (912) 662-9273*
Jim Woodruff Dam, Chattahoochee, FL, north of Hwy. 90
Lake Seminole Resource Management (912) 662-2001
Open Daily *Admission FREE*

WOODRUFF DAM SELF-GUIDE TOUR

You **DRIVE** *atop the long dike* to reach the powerhouse. Walking the overlook concourse you see 16 vertical lift gates spewing forth clouds of mist and furious white water. Four gates were open on my visit and far below *hundreds of water birds* were feeding on fish from the spillways. Countless **anglers** were ankle-deep in calmer water with nets and lines "pullin em in". There are **vast greens** below the dam for parking or "watching". Inside the powerhouse are *glass see-thrus* for observing the gigantic hydraulic generator units. Don't miss the **PROMENADE DECK** (entrance is inside powerhouse). It gets you outside "close up and personal" to the wild sluiceways with their deafening roaring water. On windy days you'll take some spray . . . the experience is awesome!!! From this vantage point it is not possible to take a bad picture. How about some facts:

Reservoir Shoreline . . . 500 miles
Earth Dike . . . 3600 feet
Gated Spillway . . . 766 feet
Powerhouse . . . 259 ft. long, 136 ft. wide, 141 ft. high
Cost . . . $46,500,000.
Boat Lock . . . 82 by 450 ft. — Max. lift . . . 33 ft.
Reservoir . . . 37,500 acres
Authorized . . . 1946
Completed . . . 1957

Chattahoochee, FL, 1½ mi. north of Hwy. 90 *(MAP Pg. 54)*
Resource Management (912) 622-2001
Self Tours Mon.-Fri, 8-4. *Group Tours call (850) 663-2291*
Closed Sat., Sun. and Holidays *Admission FREE*

FLORIDA'S NATIONAL FORESTS

Florida has 3 National Forests . . . APALACHICOLA, OCALA and OSCEOLA. There are endless possibilities for recreation. Below is a list of *"special areas"* which are favorites of forest visitors!

Forest	Name of Area	Type of Area	Acres
Ocala	Bowers Bluff	Archeological	130
Apalachicola	Leon Sinks	Geological	55
Ocala	Cathead Pond	Historical	1
Ocala	Davenport Landing	Historical	2
Ocala	Alexander Springs Creek	Scenic	6,600
Ocala	Juniper Springs Creek	Scenic	1,130
Ocala	Kimball Island	Scenic	1,000
Ocala	Lake Charles	Scenic	889
Apalachicola	Morrison Hammock	Scenic	240
Apalachicola	Rocky Bluff	Scenic	222
Ocala	Black Water Creek Swamp	Scenic	1,516
Apalachicola	River Sinks	Geological	345
Ocala	Mormon Branch	Botanical	2,085
Apalachicola	Savannahs	Botanical	2,162
Ocala	Redwater Lake	Scenic	662
Ocala	Mud Lake	Geological	1,151
Osceola	Big Gum Swamp Wilderness	Botanical	13,600
Osceola	Ocean Pond Olustee Beach	Hist.-Scenic	1,760

APALACHICOLA NATIONAL FOREST
Apalachicola Ranger District
FL Highway 20
P.O. Box 579
Bristol, FL 32321
Telephone (850) 643-2282

Wakulla Ranger District
US Highway 319
Route 6, Box 575
Tallahassee, FL 32304
Telephone (850) 926-3561

OCALA NATIONAL FOREST
Lake George Ranger District
FL Highway 40 East
Routh 2, Box 701
Silver Springs, FL 32688
Telephone (352) 625-2520

Seminole Ranger District
FL Highway 19 North
1551 Umatilla Rd.
Eustis, FL 32726
Telephone (352) 669-3153

OSCEOLA NATIONAL FOREST
Osceola Ranger District
US Highway 90
P.O. Box 70
Olustee, FL 32072
Telephone (904) 752-2577

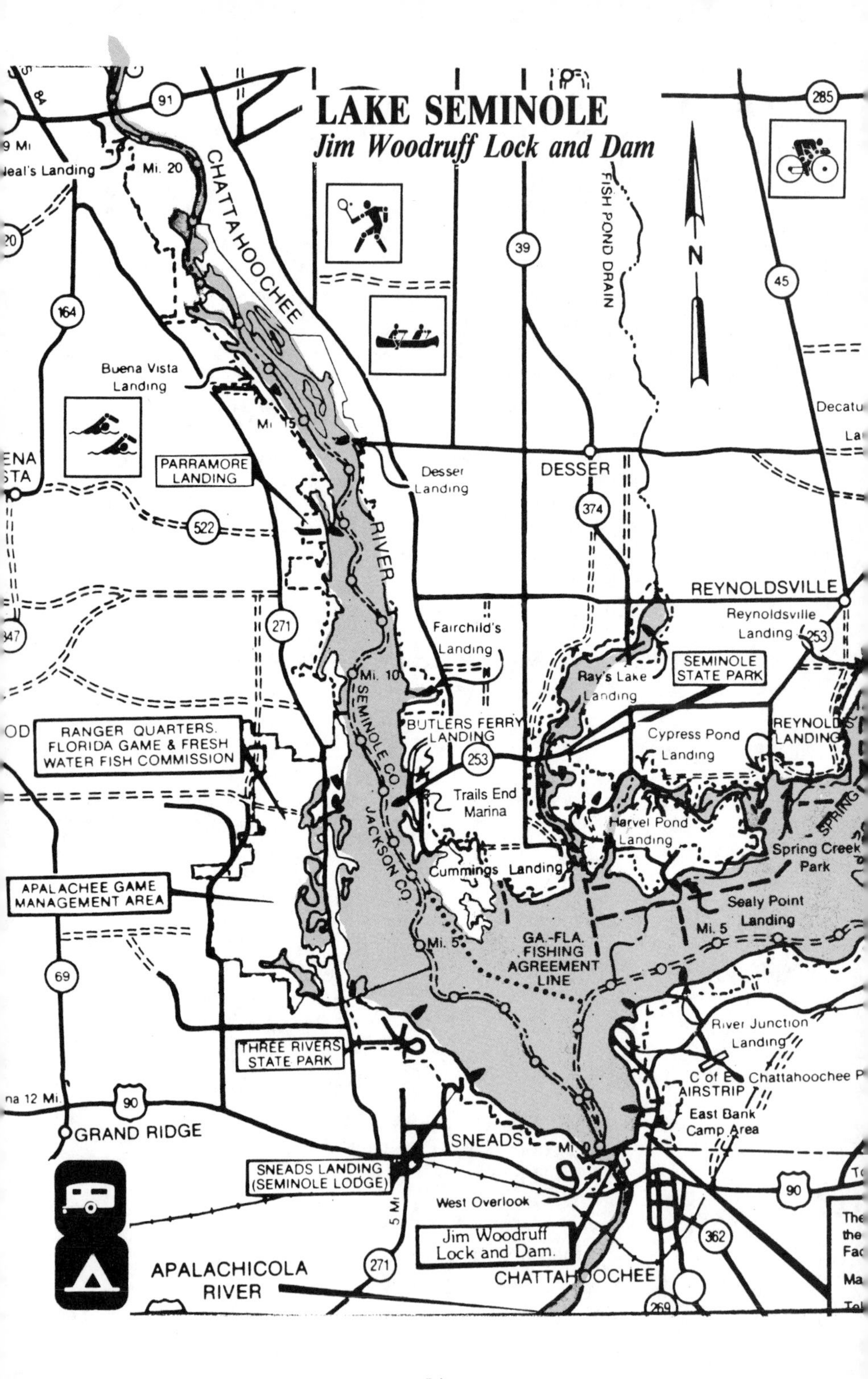
LAKE SEMINOLE
Jim Woodruff Lock and Dam
CHATTAHOOCHEE
RIVER
Neal's Landing
Mi. 20
Buena Vista Landing
Mi. 15
PARRAMORE LANDING
Desser Landing
DESSER
FISH POND DRAIN
N
REYNOLDSVILLE
Reynoldsville Landing
Fairchild's Landing
Ray's Lake Landing
SEMINOLE STATE PARK
Mi. 10
SEMINOLE CO.
JACKSON CO.
BUTLERS FERRY LANDING
Cypress Pond Landing
REYNOLDS LANDING
RANGER QUARTERS. FLORIDA GAME & FRESH WATER FISH COMMISSION
Trails End Marina
Harvel Pond Landing
Spring Creek Park
Cummings Landing
APALACHEE GAME MANAGEMENT AREA
Sealy Point Landing
Mi. 5
GA.-FLA. FISHING AGREEMENT LINE
River Junction Landing
THREE RIVERS STATE PARK
C of E AIRSTRIP
Chattahoochee P
East Bank Camp Area
GRAND RIDGE
SNEADS
Mi. 0
SNEADS LANDING (SEMINOLE LODGE)
West Overlook
Jim Woodruff Lock and Dam.
APALACHICOLA RIVER
CHATTAHOOCHEE
5 Mi
91
285
39
45
164
374
522
271
253
69
90
362
269
Decatu

BRADWELL BAY WILDERNESS

Apalachicola National Forest

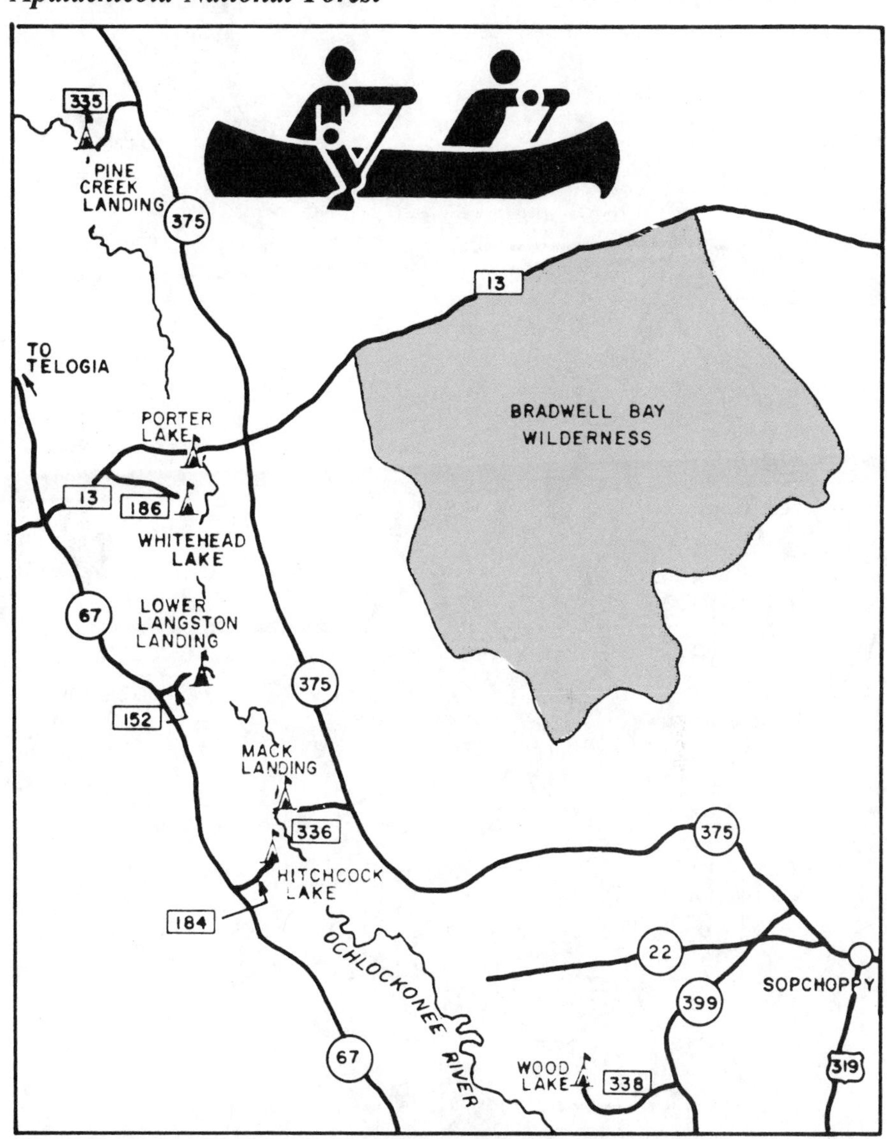

BRADWELL BAY WILDERNESS: 24,600 acres featuring titi swamps, secluded forests, and a portion of the Sopchoppy River. The Florida National Scenic Trail (Apalachicola Trail) crosses the area. Sopchoppy River may be canoed at medium to high water.

HITCHCOCK LAKE: Excellent fishing and canoeing leading into the Ocholochonee River.

Facilities: Camping (10 units), picnicking, sanitary facilities, boat ramp; no drinking water.

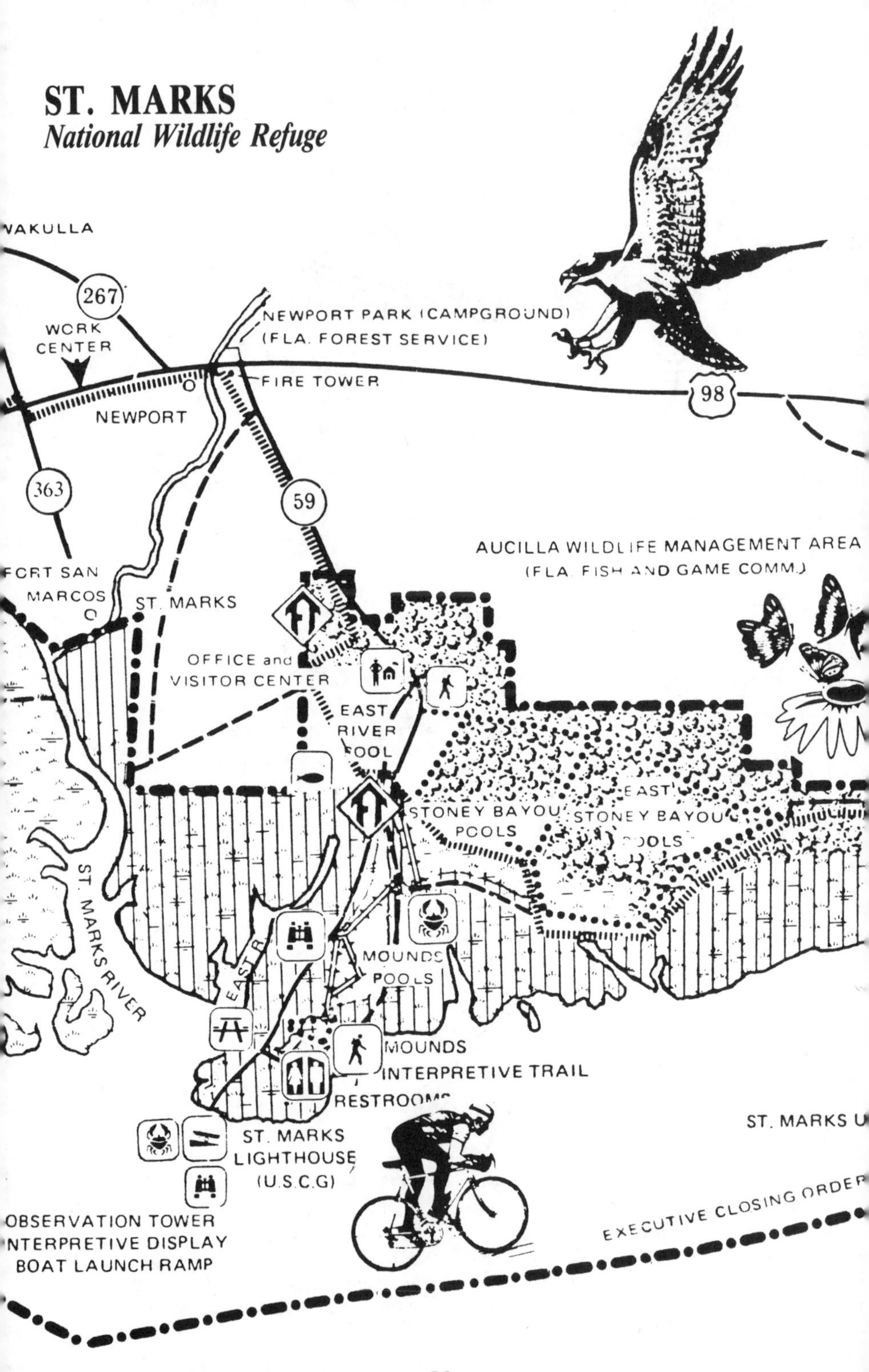

ST. MARKS
National Wildlife Refuge
267
WORK CENTER
NEWPORT PARK (CAMPGROUND)
(FLA. FOREST SERVICE)
FIRE TOWER
NEWPORT
98
363
59
AUCILLA WILDLIFE MANAGEMENT AREA
(FLA. FISH AND GAME COMM.)
FORT SAN MARCOS
ST. MARKS
OFFICE and VISITOR CENTER
EAST RIVER POOL
STONEY BAYOU POOLS
EAST STONEY BAYOU POOLS
ST. MARKS RIVER
EAST R.
MOUNDS POOLS
MOUNDS INTERPRETIVE TRAIL
RESTROOMS
ST. MARKS LIGHTHOUSE (U.S.C.G)
OBSERVATION TOWER
INTERPRETIVE DISPLAY
BOAT LAUNCH RAMP
EXECUTIVE CLOSING ORDER

LEON SINKS GEOLOGICAL AREA

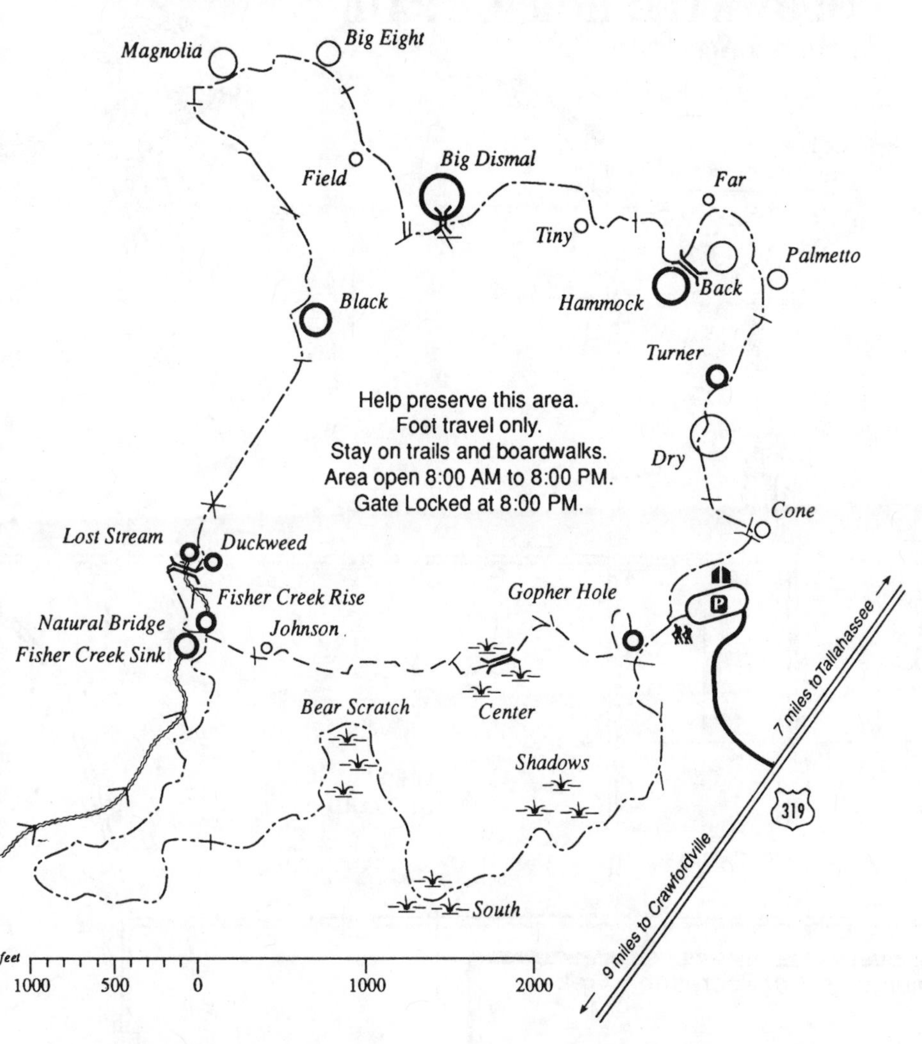

Apalachicola National Forest

Trail head

Parking

Restroom

Boardwalk

Stream

Intersection of trail and forest road

Wet Sink

Dry Sink

Swamp

Sinkhole trail
3.1 miles marked with blue blazes

Crossover trail
0.5 miles marked with white blazes

Gumswamp trail
2.3 miles marked with green blazes

Note: Average walking pace is 3 mph

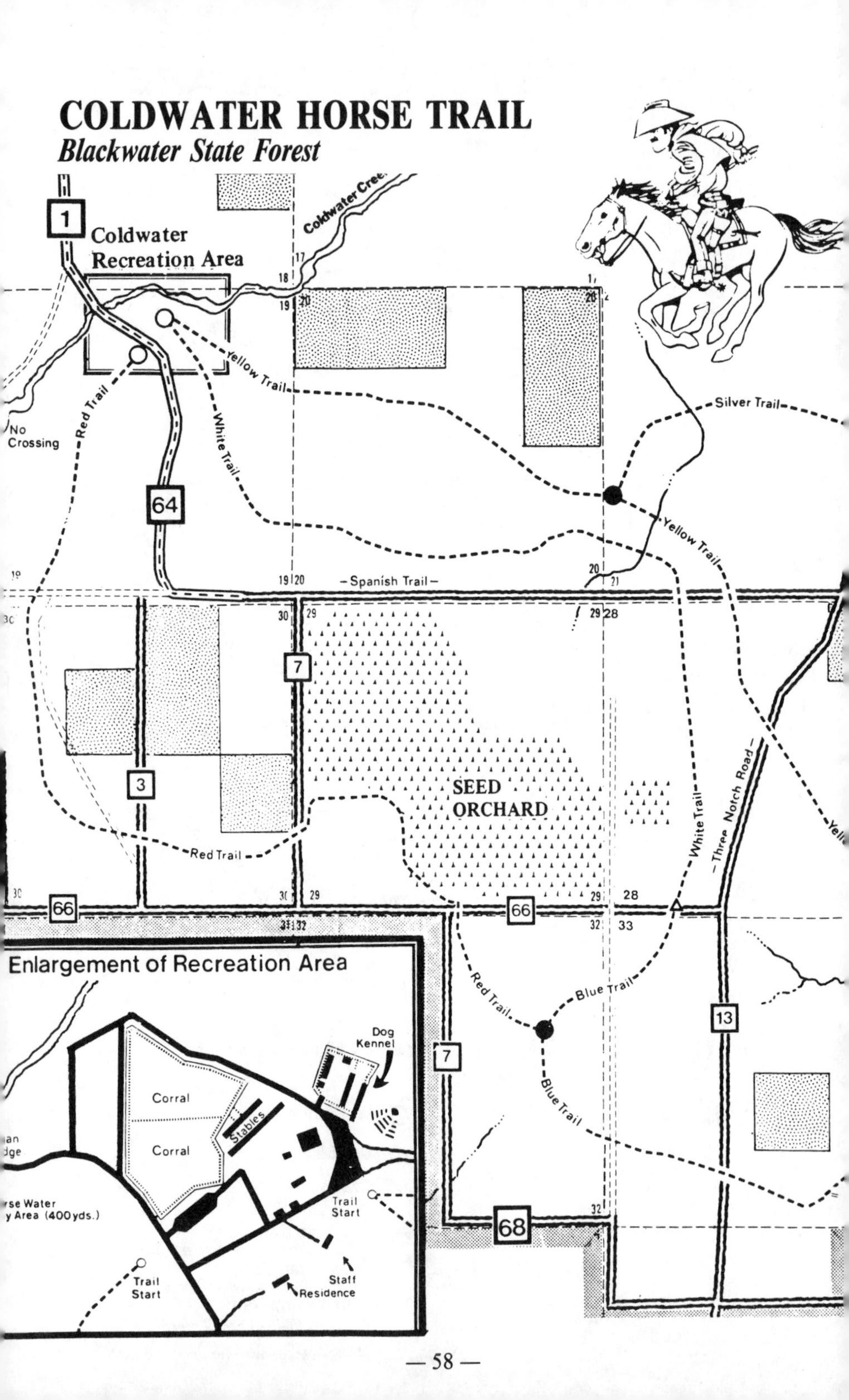
COLDWATER HORSE TRAIL
Blackwater State Forest
Coldwater Creek
Coldwater
Recreation Area
Yellow Trail
White Trail
Red Trail
No Crossing
Silver Trail
Spanish Trail
SEED
ORCHARD
Three Notch Road
Blue Trail
Enlargement of Recreation Area
Corral
Corral
Stables
Dog
Kennel
Trail
Start
Staff
Residence
Trail
Start
1
64
7
3
66
13
68

TALLAHASSEE ST. MARKS HISTORIC RAILROAD STATE TRAIL

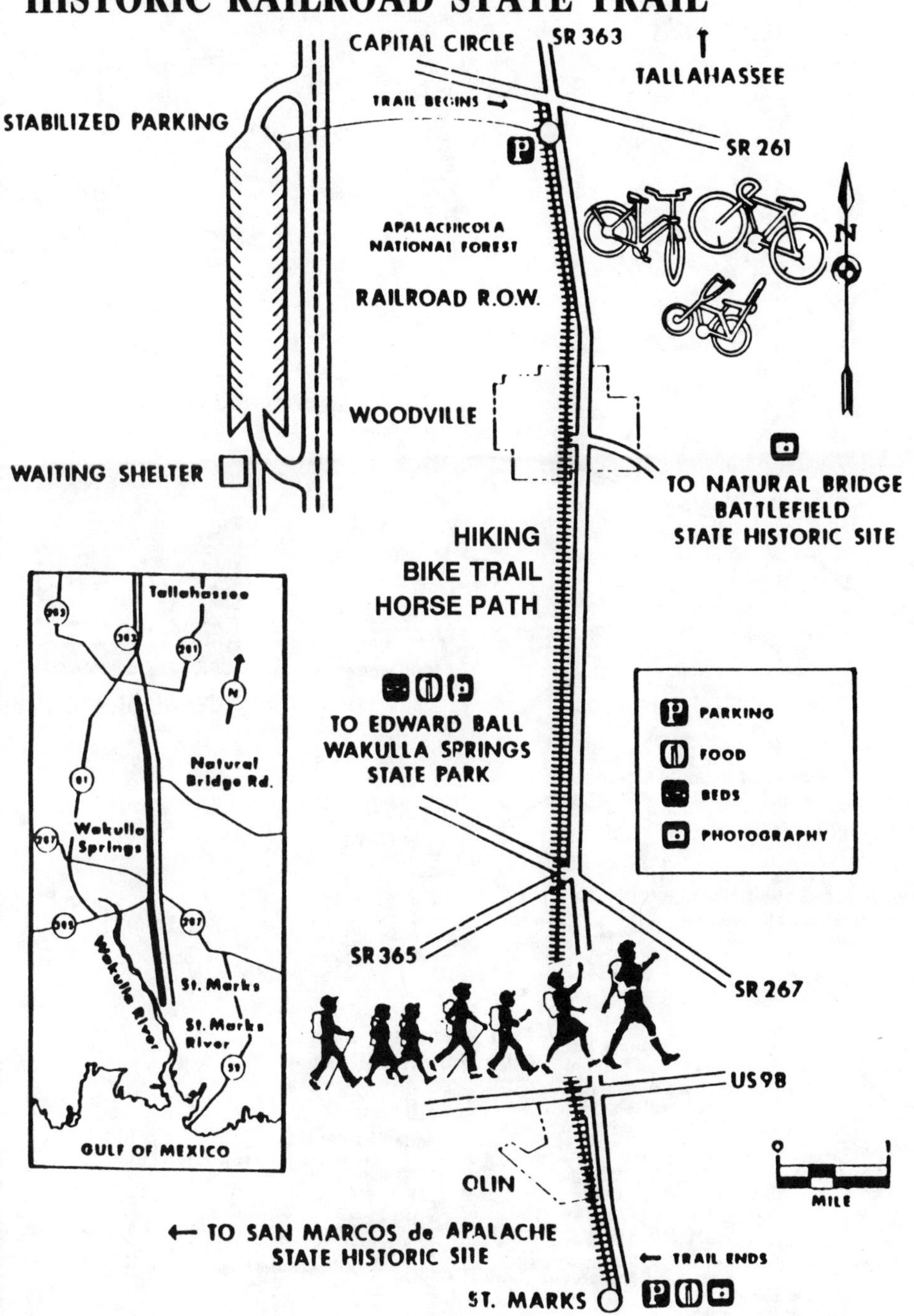

FORT PICKENS
Historic Forts and Naval Live Oaks

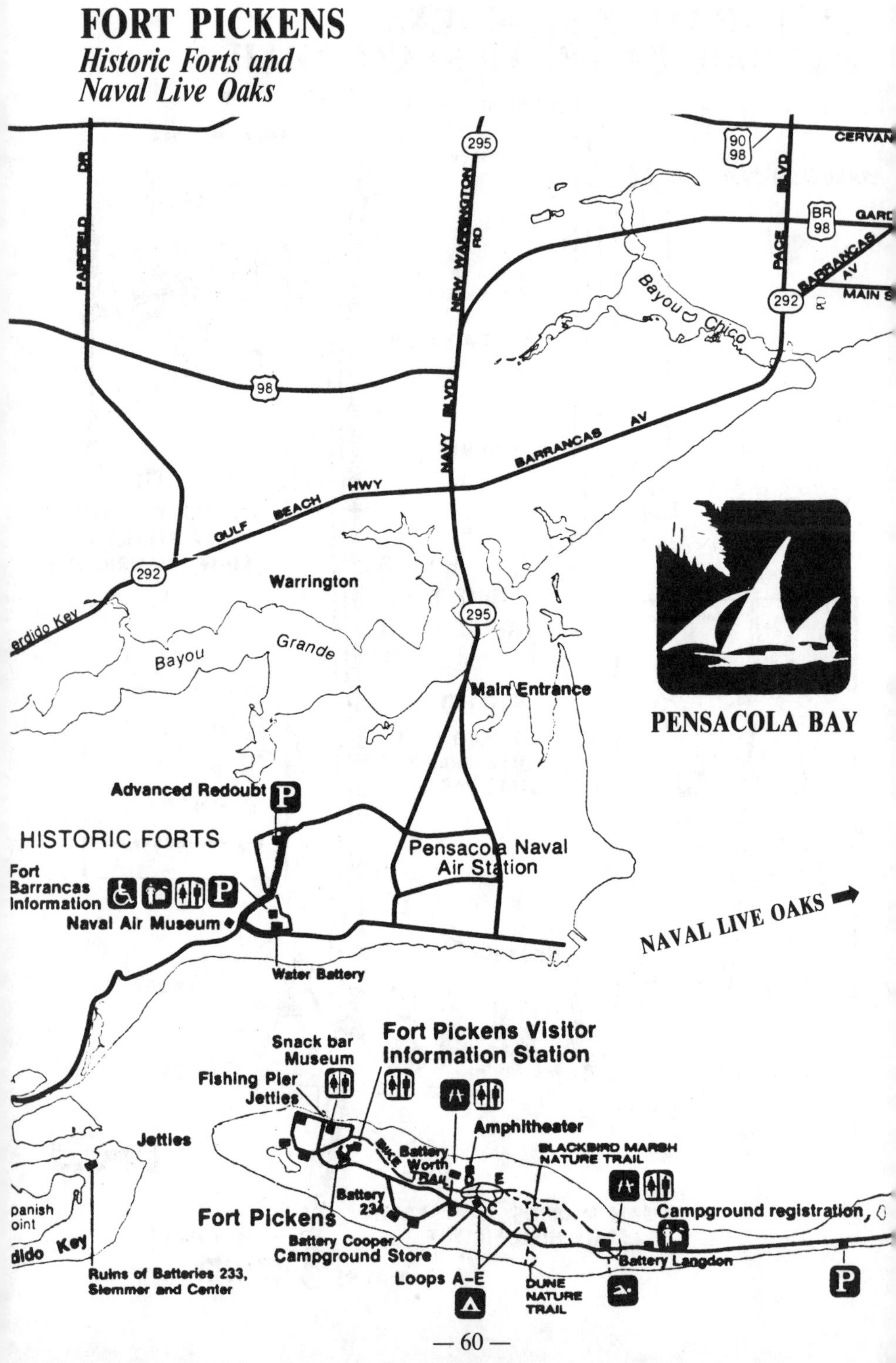

ST. VINCENT ISLAND N.W.R.

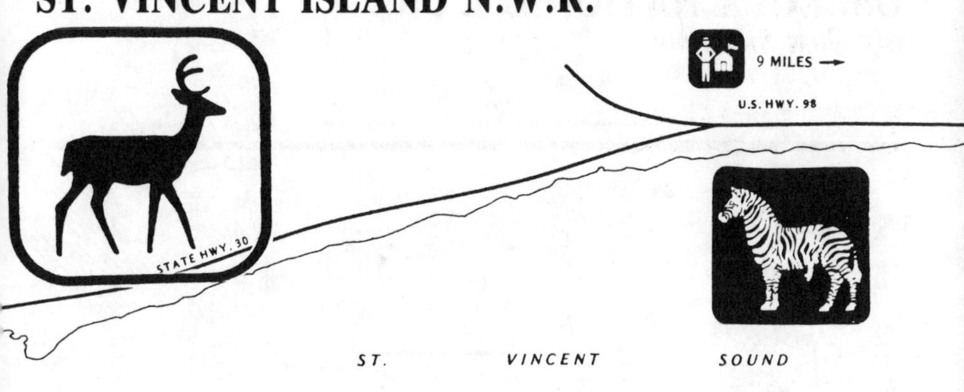

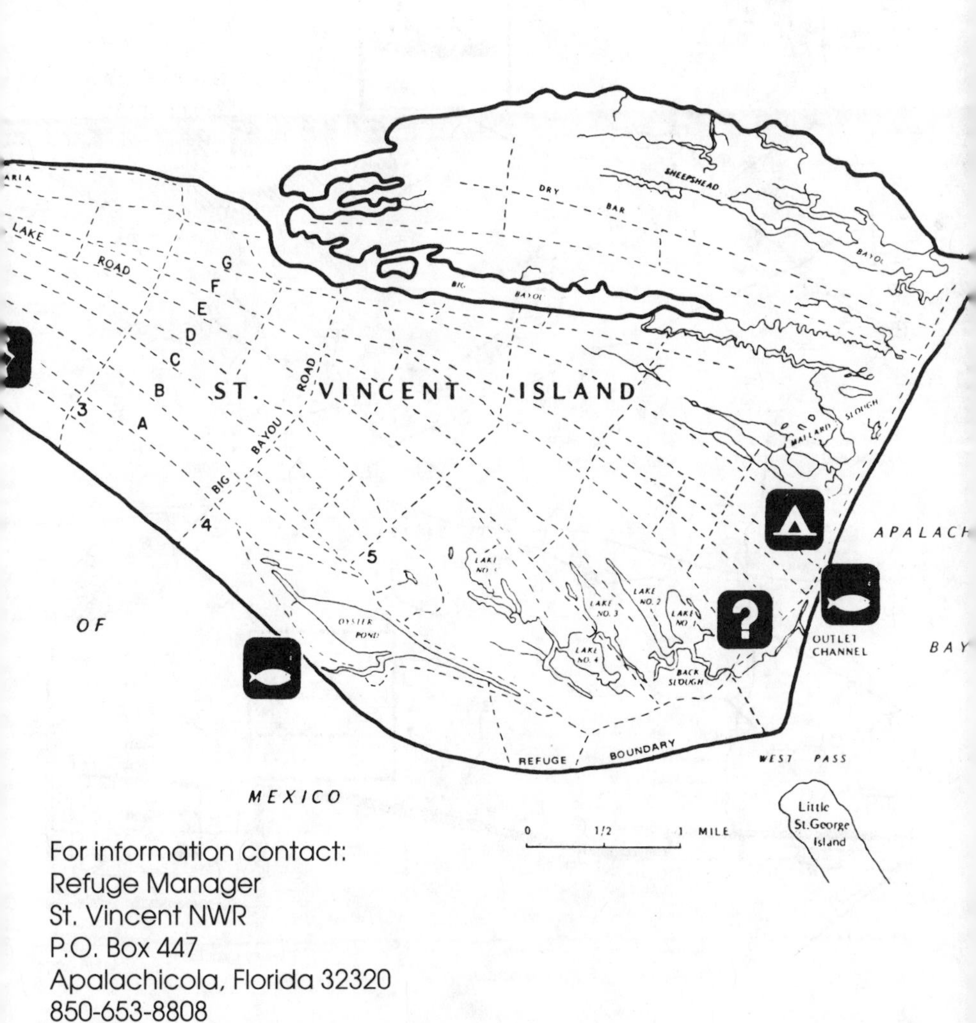

For information contact:
Refuge Manager
St. Vincent NWR
P.O. Box 447
Apalachicola, Florida 32320
850-653-8808

OSCEOLA NATIONAL FOREST
Big Gum Swamp

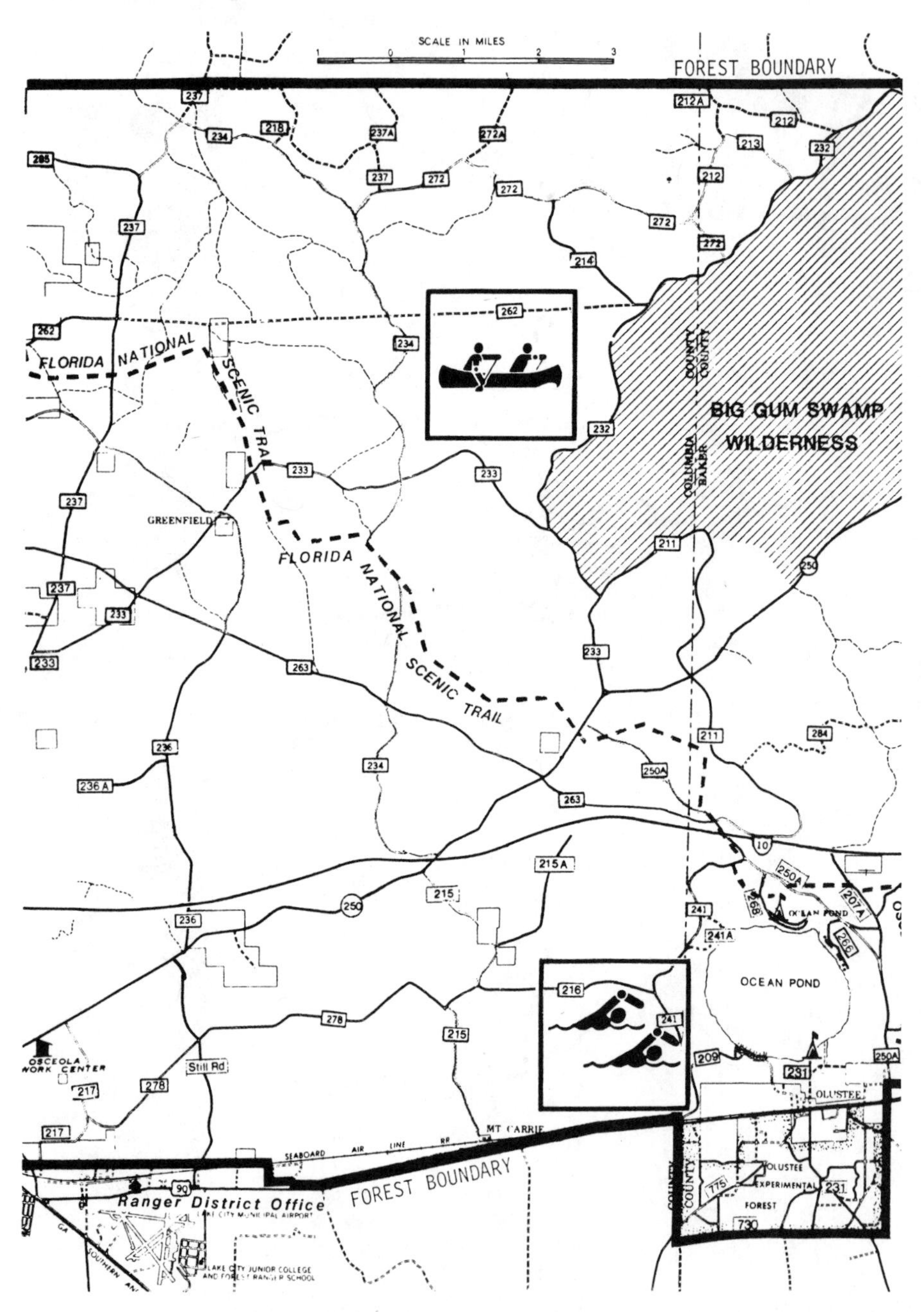

APALACHEE WILDLIFE MGMT. AREA

7,952 Acres
Jackson County

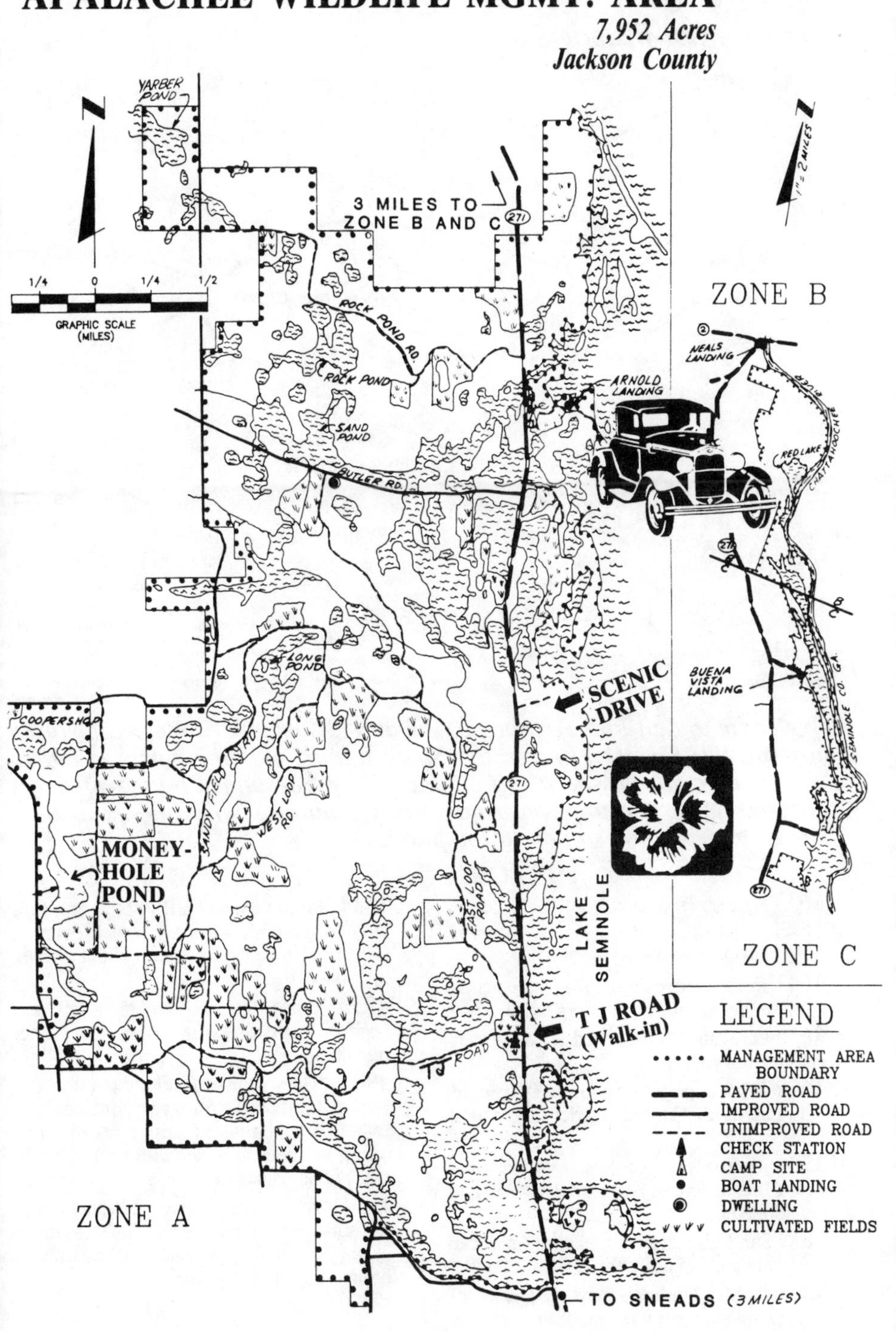

SAN LUIS
Archaeological-Historic Site

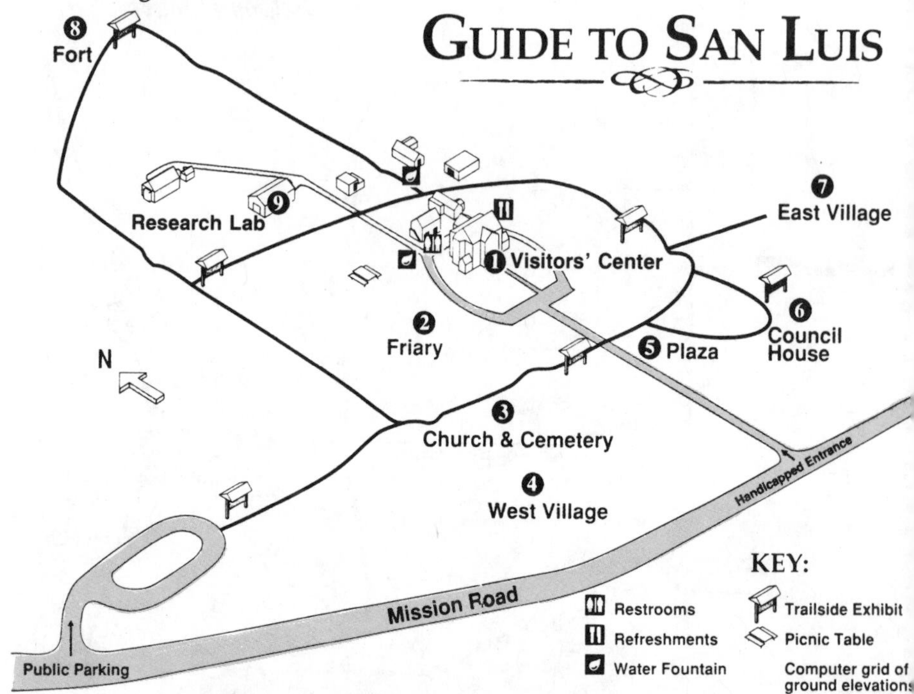

Welcome to San Luis Archaeological and Historic Site. We invite you to explore this former 17th-century Spanish mission and Apalachee Indian townsite on your own, or to join one of our free guided tours, which are offered daily. An unpaved trail connects outdoor exhibits, excavation areas, and buildings open to the public.

HISTORIC SAN LUIS

1633 Spanish friars arrive in Apalachee.

1645 The first deputy governor of Apalachee is appointed.

1647 Indians stage an uprising, seven churches are destroyed, three friars killed.

1656 San Luis is recognized as the provincial mission capital.

1675 With a population of 1,400 people, San Luis is the largest district in the province.

1704 In the face of hostile British and Creek Indian forces, San Luis is burned and abandoned.

1823 San Luis ruins are noted by American surveyors seeking a site for Florida's capital.

1855 A.M. Randolph buys 320 acres of former mission land to establish a plantation.

1884 Vintner Emile DuBois buys San Luis land to establish a winery, which operates until Leon County votes to prohibit alcohol in 1904.

1932 James Messer buys 362 acres and begins construction of a mansion and other buildings.

1983 The State of Florida purchases Messer's remaining 50 acres from his heirs for $1.05 million to establish a site for year-round archaeological and historical research, and public education.

1984 Archaeological research begins with a site survey to determine the likely locations of mission buildings. Full-scale excavation begins the following year.